The
Christ-Centred
Church

The Christ-Centred Church

CREATING FEARLESS, SPIRIT-FILLED
FOLLOWERS OF CHRIST

A. W. TOZER
EDITED BY
JAMES L. SNYDER

MONARCH
BOOKS

Oxford, UK & Grand Rapids, Michigan, USA

First published in the UK in 2009 by Monarch Books
(a publishing imprint of Lion Hudson plc),
Mayfield House, 256 Banbury Road, Oxford OX2 7DH
Tel: +44 (0) 1865 302750 Fax: +44 (0) 1865 302757
Email: monarch@lionhudson.com
www.lionhudson.com

Distributed by:
UK: Marston Book Services Ltd, PO Box 269,
Abingdon, Oxon OX14 4YN

ISBN: 978-1-85424-911-1

British Library Cataloguing Data
A catalogue record for this book is available from the British
Library.

Printed in England by CPI Cox & Wyman.

Contents

Introduction

by James L. Snyder

A Prophet Looks at the Church

The church of Jesus Christ has had no greater critic than
Aiden Wilson Tozer (1897–1963). During his lifetime,
many regarded him as a prophet and listened to what
he said, or read what he wrote, with a certain degree of
anticipation. Some did not agree with him on everything,
but recognized that his voice was authentic and that
somewhere in his words was the voice of God. Whenever
he spoke, they knew they would hear from someone who
had heard from God.

Dr Tozer was neutral on very few issues. Nobody
could ever listen to a sermon or read one of his books or
essays and wonder what he meant. He never spoke or
wrote on any subject unless he had a strong conviction
about it.

Tozer's criticism of the church flowed from a heart
that above all else loved the Head of the church. You cannot have listened to Tozer or read any of his books without being impressed by his intense love and appreciation
for the second Person of the Trinity. Anything that in any
way challenged the Person or authority of Christ brought
Tozer to his feet. He measured each and every thing in
the church by this criterion: does it exalt Jesus Christ?

Also, it cannot be helped but be noticed that Dr Tozer

had a tremendous love for the body of Christ. He loved Christians of all shades and intensities. He loved those who were well read in theology as well as those who were simple believers in what they called "the Book".

He even admired those Christians with whom he disagreed on a number of issues. He never made doctrine a litmus test for fellowship, and enjoyed a wide variety of fellowship among many denominations. In the course of a week, he might have preached in a Lutheran church, a Baptist church, a Presbyterian church, a Mennonite church or a Pentecostal church. The name on the building didn't mean very much to him as long as he found what he called "the fellowship of the burning heart".

He was once scheduled to preach at what was termed a "Holiness church". The occasion was some sort of celebration or anniversary for the church and, prior to Dr Tozer's preaching, the church members took part in all kinds of frivolous activities, such as cutting each other's ties. Tozer waited patiently for his turn "at bat", as he later reflected. When he finally got to the pulpit his first words were, "What has happened to you, the Holiness people?" Scrapping his prepared sermon, he took the congregation to the "spiritual woodshed" in a way they had never experienced before. To Tozer the church was not a place to be silly and act crazy. It was the place and time to cultivate the presence of Christ.

As a critic of the church, he analyzed it with clear sight and a sanctified mind. Having listened to hundreds of his tapes and having read all of his books, I am amazed at the breadth of Tozer's education. His formal education took him only to the eighth grade, yet he seemed to have at his fingertips any quote he needed, whether from some poet of long ago, a hymnist, or some long-forgotten philosopher. His memory was truly amazing. I have dozens of the sermon notes he used in the pulpit and none of them carried the quotes he used in his preaching. They seemed to flow from him effortlessly.

At times, his criticism was rather sharp. He once criticized a modern Bible translation by saying, "Reading that translation gave me the same feeling as I would get by shaving with a banana." When the translator heard this comment, he never quite forgave Dr Tozer. At times, Tozer could be extreme in his criticism, but it was never given with any malice or with any ambition to make a name for himself. His primary concern was to exalt Christ and reverence the Lord's presence among assembled believers. Consequently, there were certain occasions when some were offended by his sharp criticism. I think it can safely be said that Tozer had many followers, but few disciples.

He was quite relentless in his denunciations of those forces he believed were damaging the church and dishonoring his Lord. He was jealous for God's glory, at all costs. He challenged his various congregations to "seek first the kingdom of God".

During the last decade of his ministry particularly, his burden was for a radical reformation within the evangelical church. He also referred to the evangelical church as being in "Babylonian captivity". On many occasions, Tozer said he felt the church was giving herself up to the morals and values of the world around her. "We're in desperate need of a restoration," he often said.

He was concerned that the church, as he saw it in his day, was not the exalted, Holy Spirit filled, fire baptized, God conscious, humble, gracious, loving fellowship known to Christians of an earlier generation. Opined Tozer: "Until we have a reformation, remember that all of our books and our schools and our magazines are only the working of bacteria in the decaying church."

When he spoke about this Babylonian captivity, he always emphasized two things. First, he claimed that "the glory of God has been lost to us in this day and our God is a cheap God unworthy of our kneeling to." Throughout his ministry, he tried to emphasize that the true God, the Father of Jesus Christ, the God of Abraham, is "high and lifted up" with the train of his robe filling the temple (see Isaiah 6:1). He saw the need to restore once again to the church the lofty idea of who God really is. His passion was always to introduce to this generation of Christians the excellencies of the one we call Christ. Any attempt to bring God down to human level was absolute anathema as far as Tozer was concerned. The church needed to get back again to reverent worship; worship worthy of God.

Second, that the church needed to be restored to the New Testament pattern. He often said, "We have sold out to carnal methods, carnal philosophies, carnal viewpoints, carnal gadgets, and have lost the glory of God in our midst. We're a starved generation that's never seen the glory of God."

He wanted to see church services where, once again, the presence of God was so all-inspiring that no one could possibly speak out loud; where the preaching of

God was so high and exalted that people would go home in silence, unable to talk.

On one occasion, he had an opportunity to speak to a Youth for Christ leadership meeting that was also being aired over the Moody radio network. He took this opportunity to speak to the evangelical church at large. In words that echoed Martin Luther, Tozer declared his intention to "nail his thirteen theses on the door of the evangelical church." In the sermon, he bared his heart concerning the reformation that needed to happen, in his opinion, within the evangelical church.

Among the points Tozer made in that sermon was that he thought the way of the cross was hard. This was an important consideration on his part because he felt that many people tried to present the Christian life as an easy path, when, on the contrary, the Scriptures point out how difficult it is to follow Jesus Christ. Christianity minus the cross was unthinkable in his mind. Too many offered an easy brand of Christianity that did not lay any heavy burden on the people. Certainly, this was not the Christianity of the church fathers, the reformers, or the revivalists that went before us.

He also laid stress on the biblical truth that there is no Saviorhood without Lordship. This flew in the face of the idea that a person could accept Jesus Christ as Savior without accepting him as the Lord of his or her life. That, according to Dr Tozer, was a great fallacy within the evangelical church. He emphasized the fact that Jesus Christ is both Savior and Lord, there cannot be a divided Christ, and to proclaim a divided Christ is to destroy the foundation of the church.

11

In addition, he called attention to the fact that the methods of the Holy Spirit and those of human beings are diametrically opposed to each other. Tozer criticized those churches who adopted the methods of the world to accomplish the agenda and goals of God. He gave three examples of this approach: the methods of big business; the methods of showbusiness and the methods of Madison Avenue advertisers. According to his understanding of the Scriptures, Tozer believed that these three were at odds with the work of the Holy Spirit within the context of the local church. Along with this, he charged that the spirit of modern evangelism seemed to be foreign to that of the New Testament. At all costs, he declared, we must get back to New Testament principles.

He also believed that when Christ saved a person he did so to make him or her both a worshiper and a worker. He once said, "Unless we are worshipers, we are simply religious Japanese dancing mice moving around in a circle getting nowhere."

Throughout this book, Tozer touches both on these issues and on many other aspects of the church of Jesus Christ, especially the evangelical church. Tozer warns that we need to beware of what he called the "religious wordgame". By this he meant the idea, held by many, that if they read something in the Bible it must automatically be true in their own lives.

He deals with the idea that many good and powerful words in the past have lost their original meaning, or indeed have had their meaning changed by present-day leaders. He claims that these words are dead words and are damaging the very core of Christianity. He then offers what he calls "live" words for present-day Christians.

In this book, Dr Tozer calls for a real examination of our hearts. Some people simply play at religion, play at church and don't really experience what God has for them. God will give us everything he has promised, but he will not give us anything he has *not* promised. In light of this, we need to search the Scriptures. Then, we need to enter into the experience of that promise in our own heart and life, for the true Christian life does not come about automatically after conversion, but through discipline, self-denial, and sacrifice.

You will not always agree with Tozer – indeed he would not have wanted that – but you will be challenged. Hopefully, this challenge will drive you to your Bible and then to your knees.

The message comes through loud and clear. Shun the deceptive ways of the world and seek solitude, self-denial and sacrificial service. In this way, Christ is honored and the dove of the Holy Spirit can alight.

James L. Snyder

CHAPTER 1

Christ is Lord Over His Church

Matthew 28:18; Acts 2:36

Before considering the church in all of its aspects, the foundation of authority in the church must be clearly established. Who has authority in the church today? If the church has simply evolved over time, and church doctrine and practice is merely a result of evolution, then we have a different matter on our hands. However, this is not the case. There is an absolute authority within the church and that authority is Jesus Christ. This Christ is the Lord of his church and he will be the Lord of the world.

An important query, upon which everything hangs, is this: How does Christ exercise his Lordship over the local church? The answer to this question solves a myriad of problems plaguing the evangelical church today.

One way Christ exercised his authority was by inspiring his apostles to write as the Holy Spirit moved them. Much of the New Testament is comprised of these epistles.

In the apostle Paul's epistles, the man of God explained and gave instruction in doctrine, and set forth his authoritative injunctions to correct faults. The members of these new churches were born out of raw paganism by the wonder of the new birth and baptized into the body of which Jesus Christ is the Head. Coming out of paganism, they had a need for instruction. Nothing in their culture enabled them to be what Christ had called them to be. The Lord of the church, through men like Paul, wrote to these churches explaining the truth and instructing them. He also set forth authoritative junctions to correct any faults among them and to solve their local problems – as might be imagined, they had many.

Some Christians panic as soon as a problem arises in the church. Typically, somebody gets offended and the dear, sensitive saint holds up his or her hands and runs for cover crying, "Isn't this just terrible?" Problems in the church are nothing new.

The men of God had to deal with people who were offended and therefore wrote letters, inspired by the Holy Spirit, to deal with the problems. In solving them, they solved them for all time. They laid down principles that were universally applicable, for there are as many problems in the church as there are people.

Some people are troubled. They are not optimistic but pessimistic, and when they become Christians they carry their temperament over into the kingdom of God with them. If they are bright, they carry that over into the kingdom and if they are gloomy, they carry that over as well. The point is that temperament is not sin; it is the way people are. When a person is converted, the Lord has to deliver them from what is wrong in their temperament.

In Paul's day, thousands of people lived in Rome; tens of thousands lived in Corinth and Galatia, Thessalonica and Ephesus. There were hundreds of thousands of people in these places, yet the epistles say, for example: "From Paul *to the Romans.*" Why did Paul write to the Romans or Corinthians? He did not write to the masses at all, but to a small minority group within Rome or Corinth. Paul wrote to those who had believed in the Lord Jesus Christ. He addressed his epistles to that peculiar set of people within the community, that minority group identified as the church that called Jesus Christ Lord and prayed to him as God. Jesus addressed himself to his own followers, the Christian community within a local city; a local church.

He does the same thing today as he did then, only he does it now by applying the inspired epistles to situations in different towns. He speaks to people who have heard his voice. People who have heard about this Son of the virgin who came from God, died for men, and rose the third day, who opened the kingdom of heaven to believers, and is now sat down at the right hand of God. They have heard about him, they have come together, they believe and they worship.

When the apostles wrote their epistles, they wrote with divine inspiration and therefore they do not advise; rather, they command. So these prescripts, these orders of the Head of the church, Jesus Christ, come to us within the church, to us who are the new Christians.

Even a person full of the Holy Spirit may allow the cares of this life to dull his spiritual life. Nothing God can do for a person now can fix then like concrete so that they will always be good. We have to walk with God on a daily, continuous basis.

The epistles address those who were careless Christians, who needed to be instructed, warned and cautioned. These Christians had to be corrected, for some of them were in error. For example, some had the wrong idea about the resurrection of the dead, so Paul wrote 1 Corinthians 15, and put them straight on that issue. And some of them believed the Lord had already come, and he wrote 1 Thessalonians and he put them straight on that.

Although it might be hard to imagine, even in the apostle's day there were carnal Christians. These were Christians who had the seed of God in them, but who also had in themselves a great big part of lust, jealousy, high temper, and many other things from the old life. These evil things are called "carnal" from the Latin word for "flesh". The carnal person is born again but has so much of the old carnal nature that he is not living a very good life. So the Holy Spirit wrote through the apostles to such as these. They had to be delivered from fleshly lust and what applied to them, applies to us today.

Then there were contentious and rebellious believers, and some divisive people. All of these were in the early church and, down through the years, their numbers have not decreased. The Lord writes to them through his apostles to straighten them out.

The Holy Spirit worked through Paul to lay a theological foundation. He told the believers how things were, in order that they might have some encouragement to hear the exhortation that followed.

It is surprising how many Christians live below the scriptural expectation for them. They are gloomy; they get up in the morning and do not feel like Christians at all. It is possible to wake up in the morning and think for a moment that everything you knew, and all you thought you had, and all you thought God had done for you, was all a mistake. Maybe later on, you will find your way through but, for a while, you will be discouraged. Some people are like that, so the Lord has to encourage them.

Some Christians are born into the world as bouncing Christian babies while others are thin and anemic and have a long, hard time of it. So the Holy Spirit has something to say to all people.

The Holy Spirit, through the Scriptures, lets people know what they have and what they cannot have. And if we are faithful and tell people what God can offer them and what we Christians believe, they will come and say to us, "How can I get in on this?"

The Scripture states that we are to tell the people: "Therefore if any man be in Christ, he is a new creature: old things are passed away; behold, all things are become new" (2 Corinthians 5:17 KJV). That word "creature" is more rightly "creation" here. He is a new *creation* and all things are now of God, to whom he is reconciled, through Jesus Christ.

What is reconciliation? It is when two enemies come together in love. God, who is the enemy of sin, and man, who is the enemy of God, were reconciled in Jesus Christ. When Jesus, who is both God and man, died on the cross for man, he brought them together in the mystery of reconciliation.

Note that it was not we that reconciled ourselves to God, but God that reconciled himself to us and gave to us the ministry of reconciliation: "To wit, that God was in Christ reconciling the world unto himself, not imputing their trespasses unto them; and hath committed unto us the word of reconciliation" (2 Corinthians 5:19).

Paul did not say, "You are reconciled if you *feel*

19

reconciled." He said, "If any man be in Christ, he is a new creature", and he has been reconciled. If you see the first thing, you will want to go out and tell someone else about it. That is evangelism at the grassroots – evangelism "in depth" is what it might be called now.

Another admonition to the apostle Paul from the Holy Spirit is this:

> *Giving thanks unto the Father, which hath made us meet to be partakers of the inheritance of the saints in light: Who hath delivered us from the power of darkness, and hath translated us into the kingdom of his dear Son: In whom we have redemption through his blood, even the forgiveness of sins.*

Colossians 1:12–14 KJV

He has made us worthy to be partakers of the inheritance of the saints in light. There is not a Saint Paul, a Francis of Assisi or a saint anywhere that has any more right than we have. "If any man be in Christ he is a new creature." He has been reconciled, and God has made him meet to be a partaker of the inheritance of the saints in light.

"Who hath delivered us from the power of darkness, and hath translated us into the kingdom of his dear Son." Now there is a translation I believe in, the translation out of the kingdom of darkness and the power of darkness!

When you hear of the terrible things people do, you wonder, "Why?" It is because they are in the power of darkness. But when they hear about this virgin's Son, this wonderful, mysterious man who came from the world above and who reconciled us to God, and when they

20

believe, they will be delivered from that power and translated over into the kingdom of the Son of God's love.

When you were converted, this is what happened. You were made worthy to be a partaker. You were not worthy before, but God made you worthy and when God makes anybody so, it is so. You have been forgiven, so act like it! What God has cleansed, call thou not unclean. If God cleanses you of anything, you don't do anybody any good by lying down like a whipped spaniel. Get up and thank God that you have been made worthy to be one of God's children, delivered out of the power of darkness, and that you have redemption through Christ's blood.

Again, through the apostle Paul in Ephesians 1:3–12, we are admonished by the Holy Spirit: "Blessed be the God and Father of our Lord Jesus Christ, who hath blessed us with all spiritual blessings in heavenly *places* in Christ." Some people think a "heavenly place" means a church, but we can see that the word "places" is in italics here and should not be in the English translation. The word "heavenly" is plural in the Greek; it means "the heavenlies"; that is, the realm of the spirit and of heavenly things. God has blessed us with all spiritual blessings in the heavenlies.

He has already done this. He has blessed us with all spiritual blessings in the heavenlies in Christ "according as he has chosen us in him before the foundation of the world." God is eternal and has already lived all our days. He is at the end of time, as well as the beginning of time. For time is simply a little incident in the bosom of God. God surrounds time and has already lived all the tomorrows. Back before time was, God saw you, knew who you

21

would be and knew what your name would be. He knew how large you would be, knew whether you would be a man or woman, knew whether you would be married or single. He knew whether you would be American or German or Japanese or whatever you might be. He knew all about you, smiled, and laid his hand on you.

You say, "Oh, but why didn't I know it sooner?"

The mystery is all there, but I do know this: you would never have gone to him if he had not turned to you. Do not ever get up, stick your chest out and say, "I sought the Lord." You sought the Lord *after* he had made it tough for you and had pushed you and urged you. He is the aggressor; not you.

You did not do anything except go – and the Lord had to get behind you and push to get you to go! That is the way all God's people went, so do not feel bad about it. He chose you before the foundation of the world. God knew my name before there was a sea or a mountain; before there was a star or a planet, he knew my name.

Again, through the apostle Paul we are admonished, "that we should be holy and without blame before him in love: having predestinated us unto the adoption of children."

What does "predestinate" mean? Well, "pre-", of course, means "before", and "destinate" means "to choose a destination or destiny". Beforehand, God determined your destiny. And what is the Christian's destiny? It is to be adopted by Jesus Christ to himself. And why did he do it? He did it out of the good pleasure of his will. God wanted to do it. God said, "If I wanted to do that, you need not worry about it. What is that to thee? I wanted to do it." It is out of the good pleasure of the will of God, in whom we have believed "to the praise of the glory of his grace wherein he has made us accepted in the beloved."

Nobody can go straight to God and be accepted. A Christian is one who believes the truth, that there is only one door and that door is the Son of God himself. We are only accepted in the Beloved.

That is why I cannot go along with nature poets, religious poets, and all those strange people who teach how we can go to God anywhere, any way. There is nothing unique about Christianity, they say. According to them, God has spoken to Greeks, to Plato; and he spoke to the Muslims and the Buddhists. Let anybody believe that that who wants to. That is not Christianity and that is not what the Bible teaches. Anybody who thinks they are still a Christian, and teaches that, has been educated beyond their intelligence and needs to start over. The simple fact is that there is only one way: "No man cometh unto the Father but by me." You cannot walk straight out of the woods into heaven. You go by the only door there is: Jesus Christ the Lord. But thank God, that door is as wide as you need.

The Spirit also encourages us, in Romans 5:1: "Therefore being justified by faith, we have peace with God through our Lord Jesus Christ." This peace is not what everybody is running after and taking pills to get. You will never get it in a bottle. He did not say, "… being justified by grace you have peace of heart." He did not say that at all. He said you have "peace with God."

The person who is under sentence of death does not have peace with the State. When a magistrate has a person stand up trembling before them and says, "I'm sorry to have to do this, but the testimony of witnesses and the laws of this dominion require me to say that you shall be kept in such-and-such a jail until such-and-such a date and then hang by the neck until dead", the guilty man turns grey. There is a scream in the courtroom as his relatives hear it. He tries to smile at his lawyer and is led away. There is no peace there, no peace in his heart, but that is not what I mean.

And so there was hostility between God and humans. Humans had sinned, violated the laws of God and incurred death – and the soul that sins shall die. And there was no peace between humans and their God. Then came Jesus and opened the kingdom of heaven to all believers and, "therefore being justified by faith, [we] have peace with God." The high court of heaven was no longer angry with us and no longer says we must die but declared we may live.

Now, do not think that God does not give you peace of heart too. I do not mean to leave that impression, but that is not what we are talking about here. "We have access by faith into this grace ... and we rejoice in hope of the glory of God. And not only so, but we glory in tribulations also: knowing that tribulation worketh patience."

We say, "Oh God, give me patience." God does not give us patience as we might go and buy beans at the store. He gives us patience by letting us suffer tribulations. Nobody likes that. We say, "Lord, I wish I could do it differently."

God knows best after all. If he put tribulation in your life and said, "If you want patience, I will give you

24

patience by giving you a little trouble along the way –
would you like a little trouble?", you would say, "No,
Lord, I want all my highways paved."

So the Lord would say, "I'm sorry. I can't accommodate you. I'm going to let you run over some bumps
occasionally, so you will have patience." You do not like
the bumps but you like the patience and if you want the
patience, you will have to take the bumps. And what is
patience but experience?

Some believers live in homes where they are laughed
at, maybe even kicked around for their faith. The Holy
Spirit offers a word for such young, scared and troubled
Christians in Romans 8:31–39. Paul asks: "Who shall separate us from the love of Christ?" No, those bumps will
not do it. Neither will distress or persecution.

> *Shall tribulation, or distress, or persecution, or famine,*
> *or nakedness, or peril, or sword? As it is written, For*
> *thy sake we are killed all the day long. … For I am per-*
> *suaded that neither death, nor life, nor angels, nor prin-*
> *cipalities, nor powers, nor things present, nor things*
> *to come, nor height, nor depth, nor any other creature,*
> *shall be able to separate us from the love of God, which is*
> *in Christ Jesus our Lord.*

Romans 8:35–39

All right, Christians, do you see where that puts you? If
you are truly born again and truly love Christ, do you see
where that puts you? You see, you are something new in
the universe; you are something different in the population! You are a privileged person and an honored person;

you are rich and under God; you are wonderful. Therefore, we ought to thank him and continue to thank him.

That deep, inward defeat can be cured only by an equal inward release. When the Lord releases a person, they are free and, until they are released, you cannot sing him free, you cannot pound him free, you cannot preach him free and you cannot get him free any way known to mortal man. Yet the church spends millions of dollars every year putting on religious stuff to try to get people free. One simple act of the Holy Spirit will free a person – free them forever – and turn them loose. And you can get bold about it; you can go to God and get bold about it.

I remember, when I was young, I got in some kind of inward jam. The burden was on me, I was bound and I was miserable. One day, I was walking along the street in west Akron, America and I had had enough of it. I knew God was not mad at me and I knew the devil was bothering me. Suddenly, I stopped, stamped my foot, looked up through the trees to God and said, "God, I won't stand this any more!" And I didn't. Right there, I was a free man. That particular thing left me; God set me free because he knew faith took it. I was not mad at the Lord; I was mad at the devil. And it was not the Lord that had me bound; it was the old devil that had me bound.

I believe the Lord's people could be a happier people and then souls will be converted. "Restore unto me the joy of thy salvation, then shall sinners be converted unto thee" (Psalm 51:12 KJV). It always follows. A happy church that is happy from the inside out, a happy church that did not cost the members anything to be happy, not a thing, that did not have to import anything because it was there already – now *that* would be a church.

It is possible to have a logjam in the church. One or two logs get crossed, somebody gets offended and there we are, log jammed. The work of God cannot go on, but the Holy Spirit is wonderfully able to find what that problem is. The preacher does not know – he is as innocent as a newborn baby in arms – but the Holy Spirit knows and so he finds that person and, if he can get the cooperation of the person that has the issue, away it goes and the blessing of God comes.

Jesus Christ exercises absolute authority over the Scriptures written by people who were moved by the Holy Spirit. Every problem in the church from the day of Pentecost to this very hour is addressed in that marvelous book we call the Word of God.

HOW FIRM A FOUNDATION

How firm a foundation, ye saints of the Lord
Is laid for your faith in his excellent word!
What more can he say than to you he hath said,
To you who for refuge to Jesus have fled?

Fear not; I am with thee, oh, be not dismayed,
For I am thy God, and will still give thee aid.
I'll strengthen thee, help thee, and cause thee to stand,
Upheld by my gracious, omnipotent hand.

When through the deep waters I call thee to go,
The rivers of sorrow shall not overflow;

For I will be with thee thy trials to bless,
And sanctify to thee thy deepest distress.

When through fiery trials thy pathway shall lie,
My grace, all-sufficient, shall be thy supply.
The flames shall not harm thee; I only design
Thy dross to consume and thy gold to refine.

The soul that on Jesus hath leaned for repose,
I will not, I will not desert to its foes;
That soul, though all hell should endeavor to shake,
I'll never, no never, no never forsake.

Attributed to John Keith (1787)

CHAPTER 2

The Relevant Authority of the Word of God

In the church, supreme authority resides in God and in him alone. This is emphatically declared in both the Old and the New Testament and has been the unanimous belief of Christians throughout the centuries. Nothing has changed to negate this in any degree.

God possesses supreme authority for certain reasons; one of these being his eternal nature. God was before all authorities.

I do not say that there are no other authorities; I well know that there are. But God was before all authorities. Lords, kings, emperors and potentates have a certain authority, but theirs is late in time, and is borrowed from God and therefore temporary. Whatever is temporary cannot be final and supreme.

There is another kind of authority possessed by prophets, apostles, popes, bishops and religious sages. If they are good men, they have borrowed their authority and if they are bad, they've usurped it. But they have it all right; nobody can doubt it. My contention is this: anything we cannot keep cannot be final. We can have it for a little while, but not for very long. We all surrender to man's final fate, which is death.

Over against the transitory, passing, relative and

tentative authority of prophets, apostles, kings, popes, emperors, bishops, presidents and all the rest, stand these awesome words:

> *Thou, Lord, in the beginning hast laid the foundation of the earth; and the heavens are the work of thine hands; They shall perish; but thou remainest; and they all shall wax old as doth a garment; And as a vesture shalt thou fold them up, and they shall be changed: but thou art the same, and thy years fail not.*

Hebrews 1:10–12 KJV

Before the world was, God was, and when the worlds have burnt themselves out, God will remain the supreme authority.

Some of God's attributes, such as love, kindness, compassion, pity, holiness and righteousness, God can share with his people. But there are other attributes so divine that God cannot share them. Self-existence is one, sovereignty is another, omniscience is another and all-wisdom is another. These declare God to have all the authority that there is.

I saw a cartoon in a religious magazine showing Martin Luther standing up with great dignity saying, "I can do nothing else; here I stand."

Then it showed a whole herd of little creatures all running towards Rome saying, "Here we go."

Luther said, "Here I stand", and they said, "Here we go."

And as they go, they are tramping his 95 theses under their feet.

I tell you, it is hard to stand and say, "Here I stand", but it is easy to follow the crowd. All we have to do is keep the holy neck of the pastor just ahead of us in sight. Keep right after him; pay no attention to where he is going.

God Almighty is a sovereign God because he is self-existent, he is sovereign, he is omniscient and he stands absolutely. It would be great if we Protestants would remember that.

The Bible is a vehicle of God's authority. It is referred to as the Book of Books. In the book itself, it's called the Book of the Lord, the Good Word of God, the Holy Writings, the Law of the Lord, the Word of Christ, the Oracles of God, the Word of Life and the Word of Truth. These are descriptions of the Word through which God utters his authority. This Word is said to be God-breathed, indestructible and eternal.

In the Word, we have a Unique Thing. It is different from and transcendent beyond all other books. It is uncompromising, authoritative, awesome and eternal and it is through the Word that God exercises his supreme, self-bestowed authority – he never took his authority from men for no one can bestow sovereignty upon the sovereign God.

"The word that I have spoken," said Jesus, "the same shall judge him in the last day" (John 12:48 KJV). Is it any wonder then that the prophet says, "O earth, earth, earth, hear the word of the Lord" (Jeremiah 22:29 KJV)? God's uttered Word: this is what we have here, and it is through God's uttered Word that he exercises his authority. It is the nature of God to express himself and so he

31

utters himself forth and what he utters comes to the mind of mankind.

Some people are so ponderously intellectual that this bothers them, but it does not bother me at all. I believe that the infinite God can speak to finite man. I do not believe there is any uncrossable bridge when the infinite Creator determines that he is going to utter forth his authoritative Word. He can do it, and in this uttered Word is sovereign authority with the power of life and death. The Scripture declares that the gospel is the Word of Life, and the day will come when every "t" will be crossed and every "i" will be dotted and there will not be one iota of God's mighty Word which has not come to pass.

There is a beautiful expression taken, not from the sacred Scriptures, but from a book that is very close to them. It bears the same relation to the holy, inspired Word that a good devotional book bears to the New Testament. I refer to the Wisdom of Solomon. There the writer says this about the Word of God:

> *For while all things were in quiet silence, and that night was in the midst of her swift course, thine Almighty word leaped down from heaven out of thy royal throne, as a fierce man of war into the midst of a land of destruction, And brought thine unfeigned commandment as a sharp sword, and standing up filled all things with death; and it touched the heaven, but it stood upon the earth.*

Wisdom 18:14–16 KJV (Apocrypha)

When I read it, I marked the expression, "thine almighty word leaped down from heaven", for it dramatizes the way the Word came to man from the royal throne that never was built because it was always there: the throne upon which sits the mighty and almighty God. This Word comes down like a fierce man of war into the midst of the land of destruction.

That is why I do not like to see man tinker with the Word of God. That is why I do not like to see editors, annotators and translators who, in irreverence and carelessness and sometimes for money, make up new translations. This almighty Word leaped down from the royal throne and I have to be careful because it is that unique will of God revealed to me. It is God uttering forth his sovereign authority through printed words that I can get hold of.

These words are said to be lively, dynamic and creative. When God spoke, it was done and when he commanded it, it stood forth; creation came by his Word. For that reason, we should never think of God as getting down on his knees and working on a piece of clay like a potter. All that is a beautiful figure of speech, but the fact is that God *spoke*, back in the first chapter of Genesis: "God said, 'Let there be light': and there was light. ... God said, 'Let the earth bring forth' ..., and the earth brought forth." Whatever God *said*, happened. There will be a day when we will see that every Word God speaks will come to pass. This almighty Word that leaped down from heaven out of the royal throne is a fierce "man-o'-war", filled with life and dynamic, creative power. God creates new men through the truth. The day will be when Jesus

Christ will call all the nations before him and he will do it by his Word.

God's Word is both our terror and our hope. It both kills and brings alive. If we engage it in faith, humility and obedience, it gives life and it cleanses, feeds and defends. If we will close it in unbelief, ignore it, or resist it, it will accuse us before the God who gave it, for it is the living Word of God. We dare not resist it nor argue it down.

Some people believe part of it but do not believe the other part. They say, "If it inspires me, it is inspired and if it does not inspire me, it is simply old history and tradition."

I believe this is the uttered Word of the living God, and when we get into the meaning of it and know what God is uttering forth, it has power to kill those who resist and it has power to bring life to those who believe. "The Lord hath made bare his holy arm ... [but] who has believed our report? And to whom is the arm of the Lord revealed?" (Isaiah 52:10; 53:1 KJV). Unbelief will paralyze the arm of the man who is filled with unbelief, while that same arm of the Lord, far from being paralyzed, is working for the salvation of men.

Where can we see this awesome power of the Word of God? Years ago, missionaries went to some mountain in Irian Jaya to live among people of a Stone Age culture. For a long time, they thought that these people would not be converted at all, because nobody there knew the Word of God or even knew there was a God.

When the missionaries first went there, they said to

the Stone Age people, "We come to you preaching God, your Creator."

And the tribespeople said, "We're not created; we came up out of the river."

According to their tradition, they had come up out of the river; however, they had been too busy killing each other to sit down and ask who had made the river.

One missionary went to work on the tribe's language, which had never before been reduced to writing. They had no grammar and no lexicon, no dictionary or list of words. Patiently the missionary sat by the hour, cupping his ear while getting the people to talk. He listened carefully to the diversity of sounds and then put the words down. That is how they got the word "money" and the word for "God": by listening.

Then the missionaries began preaching the gospel of Jesus and at last, after thousands of years of silence, his sovereign Word was uttered forth in the guttural language of the primitive Dani tribe. Because the Word of God was being preached, the tribe believed Jesus Christ, were converted and are walking in the light the best they know. Instead of the sex-related songs of the days gone by, they now sing the best they can. They knew nothing about music. They would sing simply by imitating what they heard; now they sing the songs of Zion and get the mighty Word of God. It is a strong Word, a Unique Thing; there is power in it and, when I believe it and engage it, and it engages me, something happens: the eternal God does an eternal act.

God's authoritative Word sounds in warning and invitation. Go to your Bible and you will hear God give such warnings as: "The soul that sinneth, it shall die" (Ezekiel 18:4 KJV); "The wicked shall be turned into hell, and all the nations that forget God" (Psalm 9:17 KJV); "...that soul shall be cut off from his people" (Genesis 17:14 KJV); "Except a man be born again, he cannot see the kingdom of God" (John 3:3 KJV); "... except ye repent, ye shall all likewise perish" (Luke 13:3 KJV); "Not everyone that saith unto me 'Lord, Lord' shall enter into the kingdom of heaven; but he that doeth the will of my Father" (Matthew 7:21 KJV); "But ... the unbelieving ... and whoremongers ... and idolaters ... and all liars, shall have their part in the lake which burneth with fire" (Revelation 22:8 KJV); "... there shall be wailing and gnashing of teeth" (Matthew 13:42 KJV). These are the awful words of God. In this authoritative utterance, he is speaking forth this Unique Thing.

Nobody dares rise and say, "Let us explain this in the light of what Plato said." I do not care what Plato said. I have read Plato off and on, but I do not care what Plato says when God says, "The soul that sinneth, it shall die." Let Plato kneel before the authoritative Word of God.

God has spoken his authority through his Word. Let no pope rise and say, "We'll explain that in the light of what Father So-and-so said." Let Father So-and-so be still. His mouth will soon be stuffed with dust. And let everybody keep still while God Almighty speaks. "O earth, earth, earth, hear the word of the Lord" (Jeremiah 22:29 KJV). "Hear, O heavens, and give ear, O earth: for the Lord hath spoken."

It is also a Word of invitation – the beautiful invitation of the Word of God. This is not the result of a group of religious people meeting together, having a board meeting and deciding that they are going to say a word of invitation. No, God Almighty said it. He spoke it out of heaven; it leaped down as a strong man in the night and filled the earth with the sound of his voice.

God says, "Let [the wicked] return unto the Lord, and he will have mercy upon him" (Isaiah 55:7 KJV).

The Word of the Lord says, "Come unto me, all ye that labour and are heavy laden, and I will give you rest"(Matthew 11:28 KJV).

The Word of the Lord says, "... if thou shalt confess with thy mouth on the Lord Jesus, and shalt believe in thine heart that God hath raised him from the dead, thou shalt be saved" (Romans 10:9 KJV).

The Word says, "For by grace are ye saved through faith; ... and not of works" and "O Lord ... there is forgiveness with thee" (Psalm 130:4 KV) and "If we confess our sins, he is faithful and just to forgive us our sins and to cleanse us from all unrighteousness"(1 John 1:9).

Here is the authoritative voice that needs no editing, no interrupting, no explaining; it only needs to be released.

Charles H. Spurgeon, the preacher from London, was invited once to come to the United States to give a series of ten lectures in defense of the Bible. He wired back, "I will not come. The Bible needs no defense." Turn it loose and, like a lion, it will defend itself. I believe that and I believe the Word of God needs no defense. We only need to preach it.

We are on our haunches now, fighting a rearguard action, before the Neo-Orthodox and the liberals and the World Council of Churches and the new idea of a monolithic church with Poppa at the top. We are on our haunches now, but I pay no attention to any of them. The great God Almighty has spoken so let the world be silent and listen, for God has spoken and he will fulfill all his warnings and all his invitations.

In the book of Luke there is that terrible passage: "The rich man died ... and in hell he lift up his eyes, being in torments, and seeth Abraham afar off, and Lazarus in his bosom" (Luke 16:19–31 KJV). The rich man who fared sumptuously had suddenly stopped faring sumptuously and was in hell begging for a drop of water for his parched tongue. He became an evangelist and said, "Abraham, if you will not help me, please help my five brothers, for I have five brothers back home who are not believers and if you will send Lazarus maybe he can save them, maybe they'll repent."

Abraham answered, "No, you can't cross over."

The man pleaded like an evangelist: "Please, Abraham, won't you send him to my five brothers? I neglected them while I lived; now I want to help them! Send him, please, for if somebody rises from the dead they'll hear him."

"If they will not hear the Word," Abraham answered, "they will not believe, though one rose from the dead."

If you have it in your heart to resist this Unique Thing, this uttered voice of the Almighty God, this authority that commands and invites, then if a graveyard were to rise, and everybody in it, back to the founding fathers, rose and began to preach, your heart would still be hard. For the Scripture says, "If they will not hear the Word, they will not hear the dead when they rise."

Some people ask me what they should read in the Bible and whether I have a text for women. Most of the Bible is written using the masculine gender, so women say that, since it mentions mankind, it speaks only to men. But in Isaiah chapter 54, this is written to women:

> *For thy Maker is thine husband; the LORD of hosts is his name; and thy Redeemer the Holy One of Israel; The God of the whole earth shall he be called. For the LORD hath called thee as a woman forsaken and grieved in spirit, and a wife of youth, when thou wast refused, saith thy God. For a small moment have I forsaken thee; but with great mercies will I gather thee.*

Isaiah 54:5–7 KJV

In all the parliaments of the world, with all their wisdom, they cannot say anything that has meant so much to the human race as these words. All of the congresses in Washington in the course of one whole century cannot add up to what is in these words. "For a small moment have I forsaken thee; but with great mercies will I gather thee. In a little wrath I hid my face from thee for a moment; but with everlasting kindness will I have mercy on thee, saith the Lord thy Redeemer." There it is. There is our hope, there is our hiding place, there is our rock, there is our future, there is our glory.

God speaks authoritatively. Nobody has any right to come in and say, "I do not believe that."

The Word of the living God still sounds through the world, destroying what it does not redeem. And in that awful day when God shakes all that can be shaken, that

39

living, vibrant, awesome, awful, powerful, eternal Word will destroy all that it cannot redeem. I, for my part, want to be on the side of the redeemed.

Many times, I get down on my knees here in Isaiah 54 and let this Unique Thing speak to my heart. I hear that Word as a voice that goes clear to the depths of my being, "for this is as the waters of Noah unto me: for as I have sworn that the waters of Noah should no more go over the earth; so have I sworn that I would not be wroth with thee nor rebuke thee."

"So have I sworn." The great God, who did not need to swear anything, swore by himself that he would not be wroth with me nor rebuke me.

In my own room, I put my name in there and repeat it – all my three names: Aiden Wilson Tozer. "For the mountains shall depart, and the hills be removed; but my kindness shall not depart from thee, Aiden Wilson Tozer; neither shall the covenant of my peace be removed."

Nobody can take away the kindness of God from the people that seek him; they cannot remove the covenant of God's saving grace from the person that trusts in him when the mountain moves. The mountains will be no more, but still it cannot be removed. God said he will not move that mercy, for "the mercy of God remains eternal and forever and forever". These are the words of God.

I believe this authority, then, that is relevant for me today. I do not go to priests, pastors, bishops or doctors. I go to God and to his Son Jesus Christ.

O WORD OF GOD INCARNATE

O Word of God incarnate,
O wisdom from on high,
O truth unchanged, unchanging,
O light of our dark sky;
We praise Thee for the radiance
That from the hallowed page,
A lantern to our footsteps,
Shines on from age to age.

The church from her dear Master
Received the gift divine,
And still that light she lifteth
O'er all the earth to shine.
It is the golden casket
Where gems of truth are stored;
It is the heav'n-drawn picture
Of Christ, the living Word.

It floateth like a banner
Before God's host unfurled;
It shineth like a beacon
Above the darkling world.
It is the chart and compass
That o'er life's surging sea,
'Mid mists and rocks and quicksands,
Still guides, O Christ, to thee.

O make thy church, dear Savior,
A lamp of purest gold,

41

To bear before the nations
Thy true light as of old.
O teach thy wand'ring pilgrims
By this their path to trace,
Till, clouds and darkness ended,
They see thee face to face. Amen.

William W. How (1867)

CHAPTER 3

This Thing Called Christendom

John 8:31–42

Once we have established the authority of the church and that it has a reason for being, we need to consider the church in its broadest terms. The word "church" means many things to different people. There is this thing we call Christendom, composed of believers all over the world.

The Jews living in Jesus' time were said to be believers. But the conversation Jesus had with them indicated they were very far off the track. Here is where they were off the track: They were in physical descent from Abraham and proud of it. And our Lord did not deny this; he said, "I know that ye are Abraham's seed." Their error was not in believing that they were in physical descent from Abraham. They were under the false impression that, because they were the *physical* descendants of Abraham, they were therefore, automatically, the *spiritual* descendants of Abraham. And our Lord tried to explain this to them. I do not think they got it. He said, "If ye were Abraham's children, ye would do the works of Abraham."

So he took the Pharisees out of the covenant and said, "You are not true sons of Abraham, you are not children of Abraham at all, you are a *seed* of Abraham. You are the descendants of Abraham but you are not his children, because Abraham was a man of humility, obedience and faith, a man of love, and you are none of these things. You hate me because I tell you the truth; you want to kill me for no fault but preaching truth to you. This Abraham did not do."

I am not dealing with Abraham and the Jews, but there is something in the world we call Christendom. In addition to the cults, it is composed of Roman Catholics, Greek Orthodox, Protestant liberals and evangelicals.

The word "evangelical" is to be thought of in lower case letters. I am not referring to the Evangelical Church, the denomination. I am referring to us and others like us. We also compose Christendom: Bible-believing evangelicals, the Pentecostals in various shades and intensities of heat, the Holiness people, the Deeper Life people, the Victorious Life people and the good old Calvinistic fundamentalists.

Evangelicals are a little guilty of an error. It is not quite so tragically bad as the Pharisees', but it is an error nonetheless. We assume, rather proudly and without any proof, that we are in direct, lineal descent from the apostles.

The Jews in Jesus' day assumed their descent from Abraham. Anything we are not sure of, and have to argue ourselves into, is sin. But when we are so confident of something that we do not even mention it, that is worse. And until our Lord pressed the Jews, they did not even mention it. They took for granted, without even mentioning it, that they were the descendants of Abraham and that everything Abraham had, they had.

We evangelicals rule out the Roman Catholics without

hesitation. We rule out the Greek Orthodox and the Protestant liberals. However, when it comes to Bible-believing evangelicals such as we are, we rule ourselves in. We imagine and believe that we are in descent and in spiritual succession from the apostles – from our Lord and his apostles and from the early church.

Just as the Jews were in physical descent from Abraham and nobody challenged this, so the evangelicals are in creedal descent from the apostles. We believe the same thing that Paul believed, and Peter and John and the man who wrote the book of Hebrews and the book of Acts. We evangelicals believe what they believed. We do not doubt it at all. Here it is: it is the Word of God. We believe that easily and restfully and we do not doubt it. We are creedal descendants of the apostles. Nobody is going to challenge that.

The error is in assuming that, because we are in creedal descent, we are in spiritual succession. The Pharisees made that mistake, and the Lord straightened them out and quietly ruled them out of Abraham's covenant. It is entirely possible we assume too much. Because we believe what Paul believed, we think we have all that Paul had. Because we believe what Peter believed, we think we are all that Peter was. Because we are in creedal conformity, we assume we are also spiritually identical.

This we dare not do. I think of the little song, *With Eternity's Values in View*. That is how I try to be, and therefore I do not want to take anything for granted. That is why I don't like preachers who paw me over and smooth me down and make me feel good whether I'm good or not. If I am not good, I do not want to feel good; that is

45

a terrible trap. If I am not good, I want to feel natural. I want to know the truth about myself.

There is only one real spiritual succession from the apostles, the fathers, the New Testament and the church fathers. The proof of such spiritual succession is identity with them. If we can point to ourselves and say, "This…", and then point to the New Testament church and say, "… is that", and make it stick, then we ought to be the happiest people in the world – and happy with reason for being happy. If I can point to the evangelical church and say, "This is that", and then point to Paul and the rest of them as the "that", then we have the "this"! If the two are the same, then we are not wrong in our assumption. But if there is a difference, then things are as they were between the Jews and Abraham, for Jesus said, "Abraham was not like you. You claim to be in spiritual descent from Abraham, you claim to carry on the spiritual succession, but you are going one way and Abraham was going another."

I want to offer you some indications, which would be necessary to prove that "this" is "that", to show we are in spiritual descent from the apostles and that what we have among us today is truly the New Testament church.

What are the marks of identification for our relationship to the early church?

1. Creedal identification

We must believe what the early church believed, and think that it is possible to be a good Christian without

46

leaving the truth. We should not be off on anything; we should, as they did, believe the entire Bible. I never did enough thinking or got enough education ever to jar my belief in the whole Scripture. I get happy about Scriptures as some people get worried about them. I read them, usually in the King James Version, though I have 25 or 30 other versions and I just believe them.

It can be proved by any person of good will that the doctrinal position of the evangelical church today is identical with the doctrinal position of the church fathers. The evangelical church is, in fact, in creedal descent from those on the day of Pentecost. This is one proof.

2. Identity of moral elevation

The moral standards of the evangelical church today must be the same as the apostolic church. After all, nothing has changed and man, with all his improvements, is still but a man.

The evangelical church ought to have a height of moral elevation so great that sinners look up to it. Instead of that, we have edited it down, watered it down and diluted it. We have people showing us that we ought not to be "holier than thou", but that we ought to say, "We are the same as you, only we have a Savior."

This would be like two men dying on hospital beds in the same ward and one saying to the other, "I have what you have, but the only difference between us is that I have a physician and you don't."

You could not interest a dying man in another man who was well off because he had a physician. If the physician could not cure the fellow, what was the good of the physician? He might as well have been out playing golf.

Suppose I go to a sinner and say, "I am exactly the same as you; the only difference is that I have a Savior." However, I do all the same things the sinner does. I tell the same dirty jokes they tell and I waste my time the same way they do. I do everything they do and then I say, "I have a Savior; you ought to have a Savior." Doesn't the sinner have the right to ask me what kind of Savior I have? What profit is there for a man to say, "I have a physician", if he is dying on a cot? What does it profit a man to say, "I have a Savior", if he is living in iniquity?

The church of Jesus Christ in apostolic days had a very high moral elevation. If any church does not have a level of moral elevation comparable to the New Testament church, then it has violated the law of spiritual succession. It may be in doctrinal and lineal descent from the apostles, but morally it has broken its succession and pulled out.

3. Identity of attitude towards God

The early church believed in the triune God: the Father, the Son and the Holy Spirit. Not only did they believe in him according to a creed, but he was everything to them. God was at the center of their life and they gathered unto the Lord, they worshiped the Lord, they obeyed the Lord and the Lord was everything to them.

Sadly, in some churches, God is no longer necessary. Some churches claim to believe in God, but by way of doctrine they have it so arranged that God is not necessary to them for success. To the average church, God is desirable and maybe even useful, but he is not necessary. Most of our churches can get on without God; we just give God his place in a nice way as our guest. We say, "Our honored guest is here tonight", but he is soon forgotten in the midst of all the claptrap. That is not an apostolic church.

I pray often and I want to live in line with my prayer, to have God put me in a state where he has to help me or I will flop. I want to be in a place where I have to have God in everything I do; I want God to be necessary to it.

I like to be in a place where God is indispensable to me. I would like to be where Elijah was when he teased those prophets of Baal. Those prophets had cut themselves all day and were angry that Baal had not heard them. Elijah needled them: "Your God is asleep! Or maybe he's hunting or he's off in conversation with someone." He said, "The gods will hear you; they'll hear you after a while." When he finally got those prophets so mad that they were in a state of frustration and bitterness, it was time for him to present his offerings.

If God had not helped Elijah, those priests of Baal would have torn him limb from limb. It was not a question of, "Now, Father, we thank you. You're here and we're here. Amen." No, rather Elijah said, "God, show them that you're here!" He showed them all right, and the fire came down and licked up everything, including the water.

It is not always desirable to be "on the mountain" all the time and, certainly, I do not enjoy being surrounded by the enemy, but I do want to stay in the place where I have to have God. In order to be in lineal descent and spiritual succession, I have to live a little bit hazardously.

It never occurred to the apostles, or to the apostolic church, that they could bring in a "big shot" preacher and forget God. They followed Christ. They loved the Lord and the Lord added to the church daily such as should be saved. They showed their spirituality by their attitude towards God and we can prove ours only if we have a similar attitude towards God.

4. Identity of the Holy Spirit

A great indignity has been heaped upon the Third Person of the Trinity. Some have declared an end to his gifts, and it follows, therefore, that there is an end to the Holy Spirit.

I believe in the gifts of the Spirit and believe they all ought to be in the church. I not only believe they all *ought* to be in the church, but I believe they all *are* in the true church of Christ. However, there has been this great indignity heaped upon the Holy Spirit. Some say the gifts of the Spirit ceased with the death of the apostles. Why they fixed on that arbitrary time I do not know, because we do not know the date of the last apostle and, for that reason, we do not know when the Holy Spirit ceased to have any power among us.

So the Holy Spirit got into the benediction and into verse three of hymn number nine. Further than that, the Holy Spirit is not necessary to the church; we have arranged it so that he is not required. He has been displaced by what we call "programming" and by social activity.

The New Testament church was born out of fire and if "this" is going to be "that", then we are going to have to be born out of the same fire. Not all of the books we have, nor all the creedal niceties we can quote, will prove anything.

The Holy Spirit's power is as necessary to the apostolic succession as breath is necessary to you. You have to breathe to live, and you need the Holy Spirit to live. If we do not have the Holy Spirit, if he is not here in power, we may be in creedal descent from the apostles but our descent is in creed only – we are not the children of the apostles.

The doctrine of the Holy Spirit has fallen into disrepute. Many people are worried about it, and our Bible schools give three or four theories and tell us to take our choice. The person that is not convinced enough about the Holy Spirit to have only one theory ought to go out and plow corn; they ought not to be in the pulpit at all. They may have half a dozen possible theories that may be true, they are altogether too broad and too charitable ever to insist on just one. They ought to be somewhere else.

If the Holy Spirit ever comes on you, your fear will all go up and be replaced by certainty, and you will be able to teach the Word of God with prophetic certainty. We must have the same relation to the Holy Spirit that the apostolic church had, if we want to claim we are in spiritual succession.

5. Identity of attitude towards the flesh

The New Testament church repudiated the flesh. The word "flesh" here does not refer to our mortal bodies, for God has nothing against our mortal body. Our "flesh" is our personalities, our egos.

The New Testament church testified that believers were baptized into Christ's death, that when he arose, they arose; and when they arose, they arose in him – the old flesh was dead and they were new creatures in Christ Jesus. That is what they taught. Paul taught that, when believers were baptized, that is what happened. The old was gone and they had new life in Christ Jesus the Lord.

We say we are in spiritual succession from the apostles and the apostolic church, because we believe what they believed. However, is our attitude towards the flesh the same as theirs? Many churches incorporate the flesh right into their program; they manage somehow to glorify the flesh and even write books to show that it should be there.

They take the flesh that God has condemned and nurse it back to life. They feed it and make it slick and smooth; they educate it and call it by nice names. Then the church adopts it, elects it to the board, and makes ushers and deacons out of it. Churches are organized around the flesh now and use the values and standards of the flesh. However, it is the flesh that the early Christians believed they left behind in the waters of baptism. It is that flesh the early church said had died with Christ, when he died on the cross.

I am not an old man sour on the world. I love

everybody and I am not in the slightest bit sour. I do not say this because I am older than I was 20 years ago; it is just plain Bible truth. I believed it then, I believe it now, and I hope to believe it when the chariot comes for me, that the people of God and the people of the world have different standards. Flesh has no place in the kingdom of God at all. We ought to rule it out; we ought, by the power of the Spirit and the power of the blood, to get rid of the "old man" with his deeds. We must put it off as we would put off an old coat and put on the "new man", which in Christ Jesus is renewed unto righteousness and true holiness.

6. Identity of attitude towards the world

The apostolic church fled the world. The early Christians were crucified to the world, and the world hated them. They remembered what Jesus said: "If the world hate you, ye know that it hated me before it hated you" (John 15:18 KJV).

They also heard the apostle John say, "Love not the world, neither the things that are in the world. If any man love the world, the love of the Father is not in him" (1 John 2:15 KJV).

We have a good deal of unpleasant things to say about the liberals because the liberals rule out certain passages of Scripture. I was reading a book the other day that explained which gospels were valid and which parts were written in by nice people who did not know any better. I still believe the Bible is God's Word, including 1 John 2:15, which is not a popular passage anymore; people do not want to hear it. We have adopted the world, conformed to it and identified ourselves with it all – except, of course, the worst parts like bank robbery and drug abuse; we do not commit these sins, but then the average sinner does not, either.

We congratulate ourselves because we live as cleanly as the cultured people who attend opera; we live as decently as the atheist who does not believe in God, and the scientist who believes that God is energy. We ought to be saved from that completely, but the truth is that we have sold out to the world.

Modern evangelicalism has surrendered to the world, excused it, explained it, adopted it and imitated it. Young preachers imitate people in the world with a good deal more energy than they imitate the holy saints of God. They are not interested in the saints and imitating the saints of God, but rather in imitating the world and taking it in.

I might say that the church that has taken the world in league has itself been taken in already. The world usually takes the church in, before the church takes the world in. That church is not in succession from the apostles, even if it has a creed drawn from the epistles of Paul and even if it sticks to the doctrines of the faith. Christ is saying, "I know you are the seed of the apostles, but you are not the children of the apostles." We have more liberal morals in evangelical circles than we have biblical.

7. Identity of worship

Jesus Christ our Lord located the kingdom of God *within*. "The kingdom of God is within you" (Luke 17:21 KJV). Yet some have told us that Christ's saying meant the kingdom was *among* you. It did not mean anything of the sort. It meant the kingdom of God lies inside your breast. Paul later said, "Christ in you, the hope of glory" (Colossians 1:27 KJV). In addition, Jesus said, "God is spirit and they that worship him must worship him in spirit and in truth." We have an inward worship; the whole center and core of Christianity lies inside the heart.

We have externalized worship in our churches. Jesus put it in our heart and we have put it inside rooms. Jesus put it in our heart; we have put it in the projection booth. The average Christian cannot practice his religion now, any more than a Catholic priest can, without his oil bottle and beads. If you cannot practice your worship with nothing in your hand but your Bible, you have not got victory. Nobody needs to claim succession from the apostolic church if they have to support their Christianity with a lot of gadgets, spending millions of dollars.

Most churches and pastors are addicted to gadgets; they could no more run their church without being cluttered up with a small truckload of junk, than climb up a moonbeam. We have fixed it that way; we teach them how to do that in Bible college.

It used to be that a boy on one end of a log, and William Tennent on the other end, made a college. It used to be that one man of God surrounded by a little company

55

of people made the church. Not any more. And yet we piously say we are in lineal descent from the apostles.

We have to have identity of worship with that apostolic church. This worship is absent in the average church.

We have bushels of religious gatherings, but only once in a great while is God in the midst. I would walk through mud up to my knees to get to a group where nobody showed off, where only God was present. The early church prayed and talked to God; when they sang they talked *to* God and sang *about* God. Today, we have programming – that awful, hateful word "programming" – but God is absent.

The early Christians were worshipers in that day and, when an unbeliever came in among them, he said, "God is among them of a truth." It was not the personality of the speaker – they may not have even had one – it was the presence of the Lord that made unbelievers fall down and worship. I will join anything, any group, where I can go in and spend ten minutes, and come away relaxed and say, "I've been where God was." They were like that in apostolic times.

We say we believe what the apostles believed, but I wonder if we are one with them in the succession of spiritual worship. I doubt it.

There is a great danger that we shall assume too much. We are in danger that we shall be absolutely convinced that we are the people and that piety will peter out with us. Remember, Israel had miracles in their history, but all the miracles of Israel did not keep them from the judgment of God. And the very people who were physical descendants of the miraculous work of God were scattered to the ends of the earth.

God wants us to be in spiritual succession from the apostles. He wants us to be in moral descent from the early church and to give the Holy Spirit the same place in our church that they gave him in the book of Acts. He wants us to make Jesus Christ the central figure in our church – not *say* we do, but *actually* do. And if we do not, then we only fool ourselves.

I want to know whether I am in spiritual descent from the apostles or not, and if not, I want to do something about it. "If my people, which are called by my name, shall humble themselves, and pray, and seek my face, and turn from their wicked ways; then will I hear from heaven, and will forgive their sin, and will heal their land" (2 Chronicles 7:14 KJV).

I want my little work to be solid gold the whole way through. I want it to be in my heart that I am in descent from the apostles – not as big as they were, but as real as they were and as spiritual as they were. I believe that it is possible for any one of us.

I do not think there is a church in the United States but can have the same intensity of spiritual devotion that they had in the book of Acts. If there is a church anywhere in the world that can have the same purity of life and intensity of worship, the same liberty in the Holy Spirit and the same high moral level that we see in the apostolic church as shown in the book of Acts and in the epistles, then that church is in apostolic succession. If our churches do not have it, by no wild flight of the imagination can we dare to say that we are indeed in succession and in descent from the apostolic church.

One point is not enough. Physical descent is not sufficient for us, just as physical descent was not sufficient for Israel.

You must be what the apostles were and what the early church held as its standard, and then your people will tend to be like you. Then, with joy in our hearts, we can know that we are from the apostles.

THE CHURCH'S ONE FOUNDATION

The Church's one foundation
Is Jesus Christ her Lord;
She is his new creation
By water and the word.
From heav'n he came and sought her
To be his holy bride;
With his own blood he bought her,
And for her life he died.

Elect from ev'ry nation,
Yet one o'er all the earth,
Her charter of salvation
One Lord, one faith, one birth;
One holy name she blesses;
Partakes one holy food,
And to one hope she presses,
With ev'ry grace endued.

Yet she on earth hath union
With God the three in one,
And mystic sweet communion
With those whose rest is won;
O happy ones and holy!
Lord, give us grace that we,
Like them, the meek and lowly,
On high may dwell with thee.

'Mid toil and tribulation
And tumult of her war,
She waits the consummation
Of peace forevermore;
Till with the vision glorious
Her longing eyes are blest,
And the great church victorious,
Shall be the church at rest.

Though with a scornful wonder
Men see her sore oppressed,
By schisms rent asunder,
By heresies distressed:
Yet saints their watch are keeping,
Their cry goes up, "how long?"
And soon the night of weeping
Shall be the morn of song.

Samuel J. Stone (1839–1900)

CHAPTER 4

The Ominous Ecumenical Movement

Acts 2:44

One of the dearest doctrines in the Scriptures, in my opinion, concerns the question: "What is the unity of the church of Christ?" "What does it means to be one, not only with each other, but also one with Christ?".

There is a movement, and it has been around for some time, to bring all the church into one organization, namely, the ecumenical movement. Now, all the word "ecumenical" means is "universal", "all over the earth". That is all it means, but it has been adapted to mean that, all over the earth, wherever there are Christians, they belong to one organization. This does not mean the whole church. If there is an ecumenical council, it does not mean that all the churches are there but it does mean all the representatives would be there. The representatives of the whole church would be there.

There are other Christians also pursuing unity who, while they would not say that this was their reason, just want to get together as like-minded Christians. That is a fine idea. There have been quite a number of mergers of churches in recent times and some of them have been right. These people are all believers, they all get together, and instead of having two heads and two headquarters and two official magazines, they only have one. That is always to be desired.

We also have a movement among the Protestants with certain aims. I do not believe in one of the aims at all, because I think it has already been fulfilled. Our Lord, when he prayed, said, "That they all may be one; as thou, Father, art in me, and I in thee, that they also may be one in us: that the world may believe that thou hast sent me" (John 17:21 KJV). Jesus wanted his church to be one and he prayed in that direction. Now, people are saying, "You need to join our organization for the unification of believers so that the prayer of Jesus will be fulfilled that 'all may be one'."

Some believe that Christians ought to get together and fulfill this prayer of Christ, even if they have to sacrifice truth. The great world movement called the World Council of Churches started in Amsterdam in 1948. I do not make it a practice to preach against things. I am 99 percent for things and one percent against. This happens to be one of the things I am against. The Anglicans, the Eastern Orthodox, the Protestants and the Old Catholics got together. Then, into the World Council of Churches denominations came or at least parts of denominations, until it was a vast, sprawling octopus all over the world.

I would like to say that if it were to take Jesus Christ 1,900 years to get his prayer answered for the unity of his church, and if all down the centuries this had not been answered and the church had yet to become unified, then my faith in the Lord would suffer a staggering blow. The simple fact is that the prayer of Jesus *was* answered, dramatically, in the fiery outpouring at

Pentecost when all believers were baptized by the Holy Spirit into one body.

One thing that we ought to remember is that the unity of the Christian church in the Spirit is one thing, but the union of all Christian groups is quite another thing altogether. We ought to remember the doctrine of apostasy found in the Scriptures.

> *For the time will come when they will not endure sound doctrine; but after their own lusts shall they heap to themselves teachers, having itching ears; And they shall turn away their ears from the truth, and shall be turned unto fables.*

2 Timothy 4:3–4 KJV

There is much else in that epistle also. We are told that a time would come when men would be "lovers of their own selves ... having the form of godliness, but denying the power thereof". And the apostle says, "... from such turn away".

There is a fundamental difference between Christendom and the church. What the present ecumenical push is trying to do is to solidify Christendom, to bring us all – anyone who is on the Christian side of things at all, including the Western world and all Christians of any sort – together into one vast body. That is Christendom. But in the Scriptures there is a great difference between Christendom and the church. The Bible teaches that Christendom shall be apostate and shall give up her faith and wallow in her own self-righteousness, and shall deny the power and be totally unprepared for the coming of the Lord Jesus Christ. "When the Son of man cometh, will he find faith in the earth?" That is referring to Christendom. But the church is another thing.

What I desire is the beautiful church of Christ that we read about in Ephesians chapter 4:

> *One Lord, one faith, one baptism, One God and Father of all, who is above all, and through all, and in you all. But unto every one of us is given grace according to the measure of the gift of Christ. Wherefore he saith, When he ascended up on high, he led captivity captive, and gave gifts unto men. (Now that he ascended, what is it but that he also descended first into the lower parts of the earth? He that descended is the same also that ascended up far above all heavens, that he might fill all things.) And he gave some, apostles; and some, prophets; and some, evangelists; and some, pastors and teachers; For the perfecting of the saints, for the work of the ministry, for the edifying of the body of Christ: Till we all come in the unity of the faith, and of the knowledge of the Son of God, unto a perfect man, unto the measure of the stature of the fulness of Christ.*

Ephesians 4:5–13 KJV

The perfecting of this unity takes place when anybody is baptized by the Spirit into the body of Christ. Then the perfecting of that body takes place, until the whole beautiful church is brought into the presence of Christ. This is the business of the Holy Spirit through the Scriptures, through the pastors, teachers and prayer warriors on the earth.

But in the meantime, there is a great, large body called Christendom made up of Christians of every stripe, color and kind throughout the whole world. This is not included in this description here; indeed the Holy Spirit never intended it to be here. What can we do to guard ourselves from this kind of thing in the church?

The primary thing that we need to keep in mind is this: Join no organization that questions the truth of the Bible. Any movement, any church or any group anywhere that questions the truth of the Bible is a movement that we, as believers, cannot afford to associate with.

If a group allows any place for all the superstition that goes along with holy bones and holy water, and the Mother of God and all mankind, the sane thing to do is to quietly walk out.

I have never left anything and never split anything. So I am neither a nitpicker nor a witch hunter. And I am not compelling every man to say "Shibboleth" in the same tone of voice I use. If he has an Irish accent and says "Shibboleth" some other way, let him say it. If he loves the Lord, he is my brother. But if he is a smooth talker and tells me that it is ridiculous to believe that God ever inspired the Scriptures, then I cannot have fellowship with him.

Revelation Chapter 17 tells about that great "mystery, Babylon the great, the mother of harlots and abominations of the earth." This harlot has children. She is not only a harlot but also the mother of other harlots, and these harlots are nothing else than apostate churches, which claim the name of the Lord but do not live the truth of the Lord.

I am not a good enough prophet to know what direction things are going to take. I do know that I hear strange things in evangelical circles these days. I hear people rethinking things. We are rethinking inspiration, we are rethinking the deity of Christ, we are rethinking sin, we are rethinking moralty and we are trying to equate it with what is referred to as "mores", or habits and customs of certain cultures. We have gone to anthropology and have learned that what is a sin in one country is not necessarily so in another, therefore we Christians have to accept whatever is there. We are rethinking things. We are even rethinking whether God created the heavens and the earth and man after his own image.

The evangelicals are now rethinking things that evangelicals took for granted a generation ago and never gave a second thought to. So I do not know what direction we are going to take from here. But I believe we ought to obey the Word of God and withdraw from all that deny it in any fashion.

I tell you this: while I live, there will be one free Protestant. I do not know about the others. "I know not what others may do," said the old politician, "but as for me: Give me liberty or give me death." And as for me, I know not what others may do. While I live, there will be one free Protestant. I may be in jail but I will be free. A person who believes in God through Jesus Christ the Lord knows where they are. They are not being taken in by a red herring and they are not going to be brainwashed by soft talk. That is a free Protestant, even if they are in chains.

We are asked to surrender to the movement that would

unite us all together and make a great, vast, sprawling super-church out of all Christians; some of whom drink, some dance, some live wickedly, some are mad about money, some never go to church except once a year on one of the holidays. Some doubt the Word of God, some deny it and some will laugh at it, some gamble and some play the horses, some are dirty-minded, some tell dirty jokes; and yet they all belong to different churches. And they want me to join that mess. To join it would be to surrender, and to surrender would be to perish.

I cannot have much influence on the evangelical church, but I should like to say to the evangelical church that there is a little limerick that they ought to remember.

There was a young lady of Niger
Who smiled as she rode on a tiger;
They came back from the ride
With the lady inside,
And the smile on the face of the tiger.

Cosmo Monkhouse (1840–1901)

Whether this makes me popular or unpopular, I care absolutely not at all. But there is a difference between the ecumenical movement, which would unify into one great super-organization all people who say they are Christians, and the true church, which is a living organism and which is born of the Spirit, washed in the blood, and joined to the body of Christ by a mysterious operation of the Holy Spirit in what we call "regeneration".

I want you in the meantime to know that I am for the

church, but I am not for the great world super-church. I am for the church that Christ purchased with his blood.

Why was the early church gathered together? This beautiful crowd of believers were together for a variety of reasons.

They were pressed together by antagonisms from the outside and were thrown together by magnetism from the inside. A body of Christians living so clean and right, daring to take their stand and be counted on the issues that matter, are very likely to get pushed together and pressed together by external antagonisms. But that is not enough. They must be drawn together by internal magnetism. That is, we must be drawn together by the Holy Spirit.

I love the people of God. I am a very nervous man and sometimes I cannot spend a lot of time with people. The pressure of hard work keeps me rather jumpy and so I do not say that I always like to sit down and talk for five hours with everybody, but I love the Lord's people. I love the old weary women, I love the bright-eyed young fellow just converted, and I love God's people. If they are in Christ, I love them, and that magnetism is what brings me to the church of Christ. Do not imagine that I have not, down the years, said, "Well, I'm going to quit preaching", but, as David said, "My heart was hot within me; while I was musing the fire burned: then spake I with my tongue" (Psalms 39:3 KJV). And so I went back to preaching again.

Sheep are not solitary creatures. They work together, live together, feed together and lie down together in the green pastures beside the soft waters. The only time a sheep goes off by himself is when he is lost or sick. A sick sheep does not go with the flock and, when I find a Christian who is such an individualist that they never go to church, I know they are a sick Christian. So if you are a healthy sheep, you will go where the flock is.

If you wonder where the Shepherd is, I would like to tell you this: he is where the flock is. And if any of you wonder where the flock is, I would like to tell you that it is where the Shepherd is. So the Shepherd and the flock always stay together, and I, for my part, have neither the courage nor the disposition to go off by myself and try to live my Christian life all alone. I need others; I need the other sheep, which are of the fold, and the other sheep which are not of this fold, but which are coming into the fold.

A Christian does not dwell alone and Christians should stay together for the mutual help they can be to each other. If you think you do not need the church, that is just proof that you do need the church – because if you truly did not need the church, you would probably think you did. It is the same as when a person says they are not sick and it is obvious that they are. They are worse off than the person who knows they are sick, for the person who is sick and does not know they are and will not admit it, is not going to go anywhere for help.

There is such a thing as a communion of saints and a cultivation of eternal friendships. We can say goodbye to people at their graveside and meet them again with a warm, immortal handshake at the right hand of God; we can recognize them and know them for who they are and were. So we need each other.

I do not want to make too much of the communion of saints. I do not want to make too much of anything, unless it is possible to make too much of Christ. I do not want to preach every time about the communion of saints, but I believe in the communion of saints nevertheless: the communion of the saints of God on the earth, and the communion of the saints of God who have gone from the earth. You say, "Then you believe in spirit tapping, and communicating with somebody that has passed on." I did not say "communicate"; I said "commune". There is a difference. I do not believe it is possible to communicate with the saints in heaven but I think it is possible to have communion with them.

Suppose a young man and woman are in love and the man has to leave her and go away to another area somewhere. He says to her, "Listen, we will be a long, long way apart, but I'll tell you what you can do." So he looks at his calendar and says, "At a certain night at a certain hour, the moon will be full; it will be in a certain position at a certain time in the evening of a certain night. Now, I can't come to you, but you go out on the lawn and look at the moon, and I'll go out on the lawn and look at the moon. I'll be looking at what you're looking at, and we'll be seeing the same thing and thinking about each other."

That may be a little romantic, but there is something to it. We look at Jesus and they look at Jesus and, though they are over yonder and we are here, though we are the church militant and they are the church triumphant, nevertheless we meet in the same Person. We do not communicate with each other, just as the young man and the young woman do not "yahoo" across the meadow to each other – they are too far apart. Yet I believe it is entirely possible to have the communion of saints, which is a unity of appreciation, a unity of love, a unity of worship, a unity of devotion and, more than that, a union in the Holy Spirit, which makes all the people of God one around the world.

I do not know whether I will take my sense of humor to heaven or not. I do not go in much for these articles proving that God has a sense of humor. But I think I may keep mine in the world to come and I think I am going to laugh, at least with a certain amount of celestial dignity, when I see the astonished look on the face of some people who did not think I was going to get there.

"Oh!" they will exclaim in disbelief. "You didn't belong to our denomination at all!"

"No, I didn't belong to your denomination," I will reply, "but I got here."

The look of astonishment is going to please me. I think I'm going to laugh, because I believe that all the people of God are going to make it to heaven without any effort at all through the blood of the everlasting covenant. There is the communion, therefore I want to commune with the people of God.

There is always safety near the shepherd. It can be suicide for a sheep to stray from the shepherd, so if you stay close by the Shepherd, you will not only be near the Shepherd but you will be near to each other. Isn't that reasonable? You crowd in towards the Shepherd, and so you get nearer to each other.

I grieve that we have so little manifestation of the Shepherd's presence in our churches. We talk about his being here, but we do not sense that he is here. We do not have the feeling that he is here. Do not talk down feeling; it is part of our human constitution; and when Christ walks into the presence of his people consciously, they cannot help but feel it.

I think that the most wonderful thing that could be is for each of us to become so Christ-conscious and so church-loving that we would clean up our lives and purify our hearts, and wash our hands and forgive our enemies, and love them too. Then we would focus on Christ and learn to live, pray, preach, give and worship in the very conscious presence of the Son of God's love. I think this would be the most beautiful thing in the whole wide world.

I do not mind telling you that if I knew there was any place on the earth where a company of believers enjoyed this as intensely and wonderful as they should, I think I would try to find them. And if they would have me, I would spend the rest of days with them. That is a sweet company when the Lord is in the midst of it.

THE KING OF LOVE

The King of love my Shepherd is,
Whose goodness faileth never;
I nothing lack if I am his,
And he is mine forever.

Where streams of living water flow
My ransomed soul he leadeth;
And where the verdant pastures grow,
With food celestial feedeth.

Perverse and foolish oft I strayed
But yet in love he sought me.
And on his shoulder gently laid,
And home rejoicing brought me.

In death's dark vale I fear no ill
With thee, dear Lord beside me;
Thy rod and staff my comfort still,
Thy cross before to guide me.

And so through all the length of days,
Thy goodness faileth never.
Good Shepherd, may I sing thy praise,
Within thy house forever.

Henry W. Baker (1821–1877)

CHAPTER 5

The Daunting Spirit of the Pharisees

Luke 14:1–6

We have in this brief passage a real-life drama of redemption and, as in the other scenes, the self-righteous religionist, the poor, needy man and the Lord of glory. The circumstances are about the same: the man is marked with death.

Luke, who wrote this story, was a physician trained in the finest schools of his day; when Luke said a man had a disease, he named the disease. This man had a disease called dropsy; he was marked with death. And alongside, calloused to their knees, were the self-righteous text quoters who cared not for him and could not help him.

Here is the heaviest thought to bear. We see these orthodox people of their day who could quote Scripture – and they were right! They were not cultists or fanatics; they were not wild, unorganized, unauthorized religious leaders. They sat in Moses' seat, they taught the Scriptures, they were orthodox and they could show us books to prove they were right. But they were hard-hearted and arrogant. Can it be so, that a person can be orthodox, sound in their creed and loyal to their denomination, loyal to the church of their fathers, and still be blind, cruel, bigoted and wicked?

In contrast to these Pharisees, also present in this story

is the strong Son of God, tolerant towards their blindness and cruelty. Not that he in any way condemned them; on the contrary, he would die for them, but would never compromise with them. He was tolerant, nevertheless, and eager to help the man marked with death. This man had the "swelling disease", a disease refusing to allow the body to discharge its excess liquid contents, which then pile into the cells until the body swells; finally, the poor heart cannot take it and the sufferer dies.

In the story of the leper, we got an accurate picture of the conflict between Jesus and the religious leaders of his day. Could it be that we, as we look out upon the world and try to identify ourselves and our times, have placed the battle where the battle is not? Could it be that we have located the conflict where it is not? Could it be that we have looked to the gamblers and horse racers as the enemy and, certainly, they are no friends of God? Could it be that we have looked at peddlers and marijuana pushers and said, "There is the enemy"? We have looked at the much-abused American businessman with his carelessness towards heaven and his absorption with earth and said, "Secularism is the enemy." And could it be that we see the battle where the battle is not, and the conflict where God does not find it? Could it be that the conflict is not with a harlot, a gambler or a worldly businessman but with the *religionists*? Could it be that the real trouble with the world is the kind of religion that we have?

I believe the clash of Jesus could not be with the sinner, for he came to die for sinners. The conflict was with a group of people who had a correct and proper understanding, but who could look at those in need and not care, who could behold their fellow men and not feel a tremor of sympathy. They spoke of their respectability to those around them; they congratulated themselves once a day on their creedal correctness; and yet they had no heart for the poor, no love for the harlot and no sympathy for the ignorant. That is a description of the religionists, not only of Jesus' time, but of ours as well.

In this story, there is confusion and opposition to goodness. It seems the only strong hand was the one that was soon to be pierced by a nail, and the only pure heart was the one that was soon to beat itself out and stop on a cross. And the only clear head was the one that was soon to bow in death, and the only significant voice was the one that would soon be silent in death.

If a man had written the gospels, say, William Shakespeare or Eugene O'Neill, the story of the gospel would have been drastically different. These writers would have placed the Prince in halls and palaces and had him walking among the great. They would have had him surrounded by the important and significant people of the time. Potentates and kings would have been his companions. But how sweetly common was the real God-man. Though he had inhabited all eternity, he came down and was subject to the rising and the setting of the sun.

This was the difference between the Pharisees and Christ. To Christ, sin was not contagious. Sin was a disease of the soul, and Jesus knew that a pure heart needed no protection. The Pharisees thought that sin was contagious and infectious by contact, and so they kept from their houses these common people, the harlots from the red light areas, the publicans and tax gatherers, all these common masses that crossed the streets of the city. The Pharisees ruled them all out. By contrast, they themselves were the elite, the elect, the religious, the friends of God, the chosen ones. Or so they thought.

Religion cannot be kept pure by keeping it insular and away from the crowds. The pure of our day, the pure church of the century, has had to seal up its pitiful little purity and take its tiny mite of godliness to a monastery and cut itself off from the marketplace to keep it pure. The pure, pitiful manliness had to be clothed in black robes and hide in a cave to keep pure.

Even in Protestant circles, we have to clothe the clergyman with a robe so he will not lose his godliness on his way to the pulpit. And some of the stricter sects have shut themselves off completely from the world.

In Indiana, Ohio and Pennsylvania, the Amish, a religious sect, will not ride in an automobile; they drive horsedrawn buggies. I guess there is less likelihood of springing a moral leak and losing your spirituality if you are behind a horse than if you drive fast behind a wheel. What nonsense!

The fountain of spirituality flows out of a person. We cannot contaminate the fountain because the fountain within us flows outwards, so that any contagion or infection that comes from the outside is automatically rendered new by the outflow. If it came from the world, it could bring its pollution with it, but because it is the outflow from within a person, it is not affected by the world.

With all the power of their disputing minds, these religionists watched and suspected this radical Jesus.

Remember one thing: Christ is not now on trial. Back then, he stood before men's approval. Now God has raised him to his own right hand and the message now is an offer of life. The Son of God is no longer before the watchful judges of the earth, since the Holy Spirit has come and has confirmed his deity, declaring him to be the Son of God with power by the resurrection from the dead. He stood and was watched by the religionists of his day but has risen beyond their power.

The evil Pharisees had the power instantly to make an arrest, and like a pack of hungry wolves they would have had Jesus in prison in a moment. However, he out-matched them all. He stood in their midst and by their silence they admitted that in him they found no guilt.

Then he turned on them and asked, "I want to ask you theologians, is it legal to do good on the Sabbath day?" That question had in it the whole world of accusation. He was in effect saying by that question, "I know you are Pharisees; I know you're strict with the law. I know you bring your children to the temple when they're eight days old and circumcise them, and return when they are twelve and confirm them. I know what you do to them and I know what you are. I know you are religious; I know your cold, hard hearts. You care nothing for the blind and the poor that hobble by."

Then, to rub the salt into the wound of the trembling, jerking religionist, he said, "Which of you shall have an ass or an ox fallen into a pit, and will not straightway pull him out on the sabbath day?" (Luke 14:5 KJV). They knew they would do this. They had so manipulated the law to permit them to save money on the Sabbath day, but their hearts could not rise to believe that you could save a human life. He knew that, he pressed it home on them, and they looked at each other until they could not bear the sight and looked down and were still.

T. DeWitt Tallmadge told this story. A Universalist went into a certain neighborhood intending to start a Universalist church. So he looked around and inquired if any Universalist lived in that neighborhood and the people said, "Yes, there is one Universalist."

The minister visited this man and told him he was trying to establish a church of that denomination in this area and asked would he support it.

The man said, "I'm a Universalist all right, but I'm a little different kind of Universalist from what you are. You believe in the universal salvation of everybody. But I've been out in the world a lot. I've lived a while and I have been betrayed and lied to, and cheated and abused and injured, until I have come to believe in the universal damnation of all men."

I fear the respectable, godly, self-contained people who have money, who dress well, have good educations, speak good English and read good books, but have no heart for the flow of humanity that flows everywhere; who care not for the poor and the distressed. I am afraid of aloof godliness. You lovely women, you hold yourself aloof from the very woman that needs you. You respectable men with your money, you hold yourself aloof from a man that needs you the most.

As for the man marked with death, Jesus healed him, and let him go. Christ took him; I do not know what he did to him. He walked over there and "took him". There the man was, his eyes bulging, cells filled with water, legs heavy and swollen. If he could stand at all, it was only with great effort. Perhaps he could not stand but was a great form lying there. They knew no way to help the man, but Christ took him.

He took pity on the sheep without a shepherd. He took Elisha from the plow. He took Peter from fishing, Saul from the supreme court, Augustine from the evil religion. He took John Bunyan, John Newton, Charles Finney and Billy Sunday. He took them; he has a way of doing that.

People often come up to me and ask, "Mr Tozer, I've heard you talk, I've read your books; now tell us how it's done." The very fact that they ask rules them out.

There is a point where no preacher can help you, and a personal worker is useless. There is a place where the soul sees only a black abyss, and God leaps into it.

Whoever will confine this story to one of mere physical healing is a million miles off. Christ does heal physically sometimes and he will give deliverance at death. He gave the man the help he needed – and that is conversion. I do not know how he does it. I only know he does it, and I can only point and say, "He is the One to go to." After that, you are on your own and Christ will take you.

There is a prevalent position I have heard of recently: "Religion is a change of prison, that is all." The idea is that you are in "prison" and then you become religious and change the worldly prison for religious prison. It is just a change of prisons. If anybody gets up and says, "I was in a world prison and now I'm in Christ's prison", shame on them. Shake your hand and see if there is any manacle on it. Kick your foot a bit – see if there is any ball and chain there. Look up – do you see any steel bars? Look down – do you see flagstone? Walk out – nobody will challenge you and say, "Who goes there?" You are as free as a bird that swings and sings in yonder blue heaven.

The best answer to the charge that religion is a change of prison is to ask the people who know God whether they feel that way or not. The only freedom I have ever known in all my years of life is the freedom Jesus Christ gives me. If I were to give him up and turn away from it all, I would be the victim of my luck and pride, my temper and sulky disposition, my hatefulness and my fear, surrounded by bars that I could not in a thousand years saw my way through. But when Christ took me, he also said, "Now go."

The Christian is the freest man in all the world – free to be good and generous, free to be free, free from fear and free from revenge. He is free.

The meaning of the word "redemption" is threefold: to buy in the market, to buy out of the market and to set free. In the market, Christ bought this man with his own blood, because later he was to die for him. He took him out of the market; he is not for sale any more. There is no tag saying, "Marked Down", "Soiled", or "On Sale Today". There is no price tag on you. You did have a price tag on you once and nobody could meet it.

The seraphim did not have fire enough and the cherubim did not have purity enough. The angels and principalities, the watchers and holy ones, did not have gold or silver enough. We had a high price tag on us, insofar as we were not redeemed with corruptible things but by the blood of the Lamb of God who without spot or wrinkle went out to die. That was the price; nobody could pay it, but he paid it. Christ could take this man, convert him and let him go, because he paid the price for him, potentially and actually.

Have you been captured by the Lord Jesus Christ? Have you been converted and set free? If you have not been, then you may be the victim – just a church member, a formal church member, surrounded by those who make you feel all right when you are not all right.

Do not ask me to give you the "trick"; there is no trick in it. You go to Jesus Christ as you are; weary, worn and sad; you will find in him a resting place and he will make you glad. You come to Jesus with blindness and he makes you see, with deafness and he makes you hear, in bondage and he sets you free.

Thank God for the strong Man who walked among those textualists, those Pharisees. They would have lugged that great, swollen body out, lowered it down in a hole and said some Hebrew words. They would have wiped their hands clean and walked away, and said, "That's done." That is all they had; they were the religious leaders of their day and all they had to offer was a grave. But Jesus Christ pushed the grave years into the future and gave that man a long, happy life to live, in the sweet knowledge that the Messiah had come and delivered him.

Shall it be a religion or shall it be Christ? Shall it be Churchianity or shall it be Jesus Christ? Shall it be pride or shall it be humility in Jesus Christ? "Humble yourselves therefore under the mighty hand of God" (1 Peter 5:6 KJV).

Jesus will not walk with the proud and the scornful, so humble yourself to walk with God.

O LOVE, HOW DEEP

O love, how deep, how broad, how high,
it fills the heart with ecstasy,
that God, the Son of God, should take
our mortal form for mortals' sake!

He sent no angel to our race
of higher or of lower place,
but wore the robe of human frame
himself, and to this lost world came.

For us baptized, for us he bore
his holy fast and hungered sore,
for us temptation sharp he knew;
for us the tempter overthrew.

For us he prayed; for us he taught;
for us his daily works he wrought;
by words and signs and actions thus
still seeking not himself, but us.

For us to wicked men betrayed,
scourged, mocked, in purple robe arrayed,
he bore the shameful cross and death,
for us at length gave up his breath.

For us he rose from death again;
for us he went on high to reign;
for us he sent his Spirit here,
to guide, to strengthen and to cheer.

To him whose boundless love has won
salvation for us through his Son,
to God the Father, glory be
both now and through eternity.

Latin, fifteenth century.
Translated by Benjamin Webb (1819–1885)

CHAPTER 6

Beware of the Religious Word Game

1 Thessalonians 1:5; 2 Corinthians 5:17; Revelation 3:1

The first text says that the gospel may come in one of two ways. It may come in word only, which is empty. It may come in power, which is with moral effectiveness. Paul knew the gospel message had come to the Thessalonians effectively, in moral power, and he gave as his reason that they had much assurance and became followers of Christ, "having received the word in much affliction". Nothing could turn them back. They had a strange and supernatural joy which Paul labeled "joy in the Holy Ghost" (Romans 14:17 KJV) and they went on, not only to be followers but also examples in their own right. They became examples to the other churches and from them "sounded out the word of the Lord"; they became a missionary church.

If it is true that that is what happens when the Word comes in power, and the text opens the doors to the belief that the Word can come nominally and without power, then in the latter case exactly the opposite would be true. The Thessalonians would become Christians by making some decisions but without much assurance, and would not be followers of the Lord particularly, except in name.

When affliction came, they wouldn't take it very well and would know little joy – they would have to work it up, and it wouldn't stay long. They would be poor examples, and lukewarm when it came to missionary zeal. Now that is a fair explanation here of the gospel coming in word only and it lies in this verse from 1 Thessalonians.

The second text says that the effect of the gospel when received in power, in addition to what Paul said in Thessalonians, is that it regenerates a man's nature. "Generate" means to "create", and "regenerate" means to "create again". That is what the Word does when it is received in power: the old things of the old first generation; that is, the first creation, pass away and everything becomes new. A set of new things takes the place of the old that was set aside when the Holy Spirit regenerated the heart to believe in the gospel.

The third text says that there are those who have heard the gospel in word only and are called Christians, but they are Christians in name only. That is what "nominal" means. Actually they have not been changed fundamentally at all and are still old; that is, they are still dead.

The word "generation" means "creation", "making alive", "being generated"; "regenerate" means to do this again. The reason God has to do it again is because sin came and we died, and he has to do this life-giving job a second time in order that we might live. But there are some who have this change only in the form of a name. They have not been changed fundamentally at all. They still belong to the old life, and the Holy Spirit says they have a name to live, but actually, they are dead.

This is a brief exegesis of these three great verses. I

want you to see what it means to have the gospel come in word only, and then what it means to have the gospel come in power, and to understand the danger that it shall be in word only and not in power, and then what we should do about it.

Some believe the gospel, but have it in word only. Our Lord Jesus taught this in Israel; he said:

> *Woe unto you, scribes and Pharisees, hypocrites! for ye are like unto whited sepulchres, which indeed appear beautiful outward, but are within full of dead men's bones, and of all uncleanness. Even so ye also outwardly appear righteous unto men, but within ye are full of hypocrisy and iniquity.*

Matthew 23:27–28 KJV

These religious people looked at each other, tugged at their long beards and determined that, as soon as possible, without a mob scene resulting, they would kill Jesus. Finally, they killed him, but God raised him from the dead on the third day and set him at his own right hand. They thought they were murdering a man, but God was offering a sacrifice. That is the difference. That is the irony of fighting against the Lord Jesus Christ.

As a consequence of being a nominal Christian, in name only, there is a tendency to use words in a wrong way – to engage in religious word games. In too many places today, the Christian religion has simply been reduced to a word game.

Some say, "I know that very well, because I used to belong to the thus-and-thus denomination. They were as dead as could be. The pastor did not believe in the virgin birth." Somebody else says, "I used to go to a church where they did not believe Moses wrote the Pentateuch. They were scoundrels; they were liberals."

But the Holy Spirit is not talking about liberals or about people that deny the truth of the Scripture. He is talking about people that admit the truth of the Scripture and receive the gospel as a fact; they do not deny it but support it and follow it, and would kick a pastor out if he did not preach it. But it has only reached them in words because their religion is simply a word game.

A game is something that is played by creating a problem and then having fun solving it. I know a little about baseball, so I will use that for illustration. Baseball creates a problem and spends millions of dollars solving a problem that did not exist until men created it!

Abner Doubleday (1819–1893) is the man credited with inventing the game we now call "baseball". He said, "I'll tell you what we'll do: we'll create a problem and then solve it. We'll put one man here with a ball and put another man 60 feet away from him. Now, the problem will be this: the man with the ball will throw it to the other man, but in order to make it tough to get the ball through, we are going to put a fellow in between with a stick. He will stand there and use his stick to keep that ball from getting to that other man's mitt. We will work on the problem: the "pitcher" will wind up and gyrate and throw the ball as hard as he can to the other man, and the fellow with the stick will be the very devil in between, trying to keep him from catching it."

So the game of baseball was created. Games work

that way. They have a problem, but the problem had never existed before. Polio, cancer, war and starvation all existed, but people had to create a problem and then get the healthiest men in the world to play at solving it.

When the ball is thrown, if the man with the stick hauls off, strikes and connects with it, that problem is solved in his favor. He is having fun. The onlookers hear the sound of the ball on wood and say, "I think it sounds like a homer!" However, there are eight other people determined that he is not going to have that solution. *They* are going to have it: the shortstop, three basemen and three outfielders are all ready to catch that ball! If anybody can get it before it hits the ground, the fellow with the stick is out.

We spend millions of dollars solving that problem hundreds of times on a sunny afternoon. That is a game, and some people like games.

One thing about a game is that nobody is any better nor any worse, whatever happens. If the man with the stick wins, he's no better off. He just goes home, and if his wife didn't like him before, she still doesn't like him. If he's in debt, he is still in debt; if he has a disease, he still has a disease. No matter what, he is still no better off and the other fellow is no worse off.

Even in the Olympic Games, the athletes compete with each other, but it is all a matter of games and, when it is all over, they go home. Nobody is any better off or worse off, because the "problems" were all created before the athletes were sent over to solve them.

When the Canadians and the Americans were fighting Hitler, it did matter who won, for it was a difference between slavery – living on our knees – and freedom. This was the difference between playing a game and fighting a war.

In the case of religion, the temptation is to take it as a word game. Instead of a baseball or a football, we have other little gadgets that we throw around, such as words. We write books, buy books, proofread books and sweat over books. We edit magazines; we buy and suscribe to magazines. We write songs; we sing songs. We make prayers; we say prayers. We preach sermons; we hear sermons.

All of this requires, of course, a vast amount of activity, a tremendous amount of money, a great deal of perspiration (particularly in the summertime) and a lot of inconvenience. Yet, in reality, a great number of people are simply playing the game of religious words. It makes no difference. The giveaway is that the religious word game does not change anybody fundamentally; people are not much different from what they were before.

A certain university sponsored a survey. They took 100 men who were devout churchmen and investigated their ethical standards in business. Then they took 100 men who never went to church and investigated their business ethics. After some time, having spent a lot of money carrying out many investigations, they said, "By and large, there isn't any difference between the ethical business standards of the religious churchman and those of the non-religious man who never enters the church door."

We are just human beings, wherever we live and whatever our nationality. If something is true in one place, it is likely to be true in another. So what are these 100 church-men doing? They are just playing a word game. They go to church – maybe they are ushers; down the aisle they go, looking dignified, wearing their boutonnières. Maybe they are preachers; they stand up, take a text, breathe through their nose heavily, and preach the Word. And people say, "Wasn't that a great sermon?" They shake the preacher's hand and say, "I was blessed", then out they go, and the next morning their business ethics have not been changed a bit. They have all simply had fun playing a word game.

We set up a problem and solve it. We throw a ball and somebody else with a stick hits it and, when it's all over, we say, "Boy, our church is growing and we're known in this city. We're a great church, aren't we? Let's see what we can do to make the thing look better."

I want nothing to do with this religious word game. I want nobody fooling me with unreality. I do not want anybody coming and pawing over me if they do not mean it. I do not want anybody lying to me in the name of etiquette, or asking me for money to support something I do not believe in. I do not want anybody to ask me to believe in a religion that I have to take on somebody's authority. If Jesus Christ cannot change me, if my Christianity is not real, if the problem I face is not a real problem, if it does not mean heaven, hell, death and the grave, then I do not want to be wasting my time with it at all. I would rather take a walk and listen to the birds sing, than listen to any man preach who tries to smooth me down or to put up a problem that does not exist and play with it. That is what is going on all the time.

The giveaway of this religious word game is that I say I am fundamentally different, but the same old principles motivate my life. Imagine a man comes along, says he is a Christian and wants to join the church. But his natural appetites are just the same; they are only refined a little bit, that is all. His egotism has not been destroyed; it is only less gross than it was before. It is possible for an egotist to get a college education and be a refined egotist, skillful at hiding the fact that they are an egotist. They can refine that still more by being converted. And the Word of the Lord will come to them, but it will not come to them in power. All it does is refine their egotism.

Then there is the matter of selfishness. He is exactly the same selfish fellow he was before, only he has sanitized his selfishness a little bit now. He loves games just as he always did – he just rubs his hands to see the money come in – only now he gives a little of it to the Lord, takes it off his income tax and feels that he's a saint. But all he has accomplished is what any sinner might do.

The trouble is that the roots of our life have not been changed, which is why we are half-dead. We are growing from the same old roots as we were before, when we were religious people carrying a hymnbook or Bible under our arm. That is why Christians are so largely ineffective.

The devil means what he is saying and he is not fooling. Christians often are, but the devil never is. Christians play wordgames, but the devil is not playing.

When the gospel comes in power, we are not playing any more; it is real. Do not imagine for a minute that you can get away with this word game inside the church of

Christ. God will not accept any tossing around of things, any playing with words or songs or sermons or books.

What happens to a person when they are really born anew? We use that term, "born again", in evangelical circles. We have used it until it has no more meaning left. It is worn as thin as an old 1914 coin. But it is still in the Bible. We still have to be born again; that is, regenerated, made a new creature. Those are the same words – or different words meaning the same thing. So when a person has been regenerated, renewed, made over, recreated, born anew, born from above, born again, what actually happens to them?

When religion ceases to be a game and becomes a serious reality, when, instead of playing a game, we are fighting a war, then the Word of God has come in power and a number of things happen in a person's life.

They are changed from the external to the internal

Our trouble is externality. Automobile manufacturers continually keep the poor automobile owners on their toes, by changing just one little button inside the car – suddenly a person has an old button in their car and feels they need a completely new model.

"This car is just a year old," they say, "but I've got to trade it in."

It is an external problem. If your house has one level and you have a friend who has a split-level, you worry until you get a split-level house.

The Word that comes to us in power changes us from the external to the internal. Our hopes, our interests, everything that we are absorbed with and in, are internal instead of external. And we see the emptiness of the appearance of things that are formed.

Scripture tells us that "the LORD seeth not as man seeth; for man looketh on the outward appearance, but the LORD looketh on the heart" (1 Samuel 16:7 KJV). So the "new man" sees the transcendence of things eternal and the descent of things temporal, things belonging to the earth. He sees the inadequacies of everything intellectual, while seeing the value of "things that are above". That happens to a person when they are born again. They do not have to have an education; they do not have to be cultured. They just have to be born anew and, when the Holy Spirit regenerates them, they see this. The Holy Spirit shifts his interest into a new sphere, the kingdom of God. The love life shifts from self to God; they are dedicated now to the honor of Another. They were once dedicated bitterly to their own honor, but now they are dedicated to the honor of God. And they are changed in this too: they used to desire social approval. They wanted to be approved by people, and now that has all changed: they desire to be approved by God Almighty.

As long as a person is a natural person, they want to be popular with the crowd, but when they are born anew, they say, "I don't care so much now about the crowd, but I want to stand approved of God. I want God to say in that day, 'This is my beloved child in whom I am well pleased'. I can well afford to stand the angry attacks of the people, if I can only keep right with God."

Their attitude towards earthly goods changes completely

The person who is born again no longer feels that they are a proprietor owning anything. They feel they are a steward who has something only for the time being.

This makes a big difference in our lives. It will not mean we have any less, but it will mean we will have a different attitude towards earthly goods. Some Christians have a God-complex; they are proprietors, they own the place, but they give God part of it and feel they have done God a service. I suppose in a way they have. But there are other people who are blessed and see it differently. They say, "O God, I am not a proprietor; I'm a steward. This is all yours and I am serving you. I don't give you an amount that's mine; I simply give you back what's yours and you let me keep enough to run my family and my business."

That is not only a different attitude but it is the only right attitude. As long as we imagine we own anything, that thing will curse us. As soon as we know we own nothing, it is God's. That is what happens to a person when they become a Christian.

They receive and lives by a new moral code

I grieve over the situation that is loose in the earth in these times. Today, missionaries go out to the mission field (God bless them) and have to fight, not the devil out there, so much as changing standards. In the early days, missionaries used to go out and if they met an old tribal

97

chief who had nine wives, they said to him, "Get rid of every wife except the first."

Now, they talk about culture. "Well, to demand a change of that kind is contrary to their culture. We're trying to impose our culture on them."

What is a case of downright confounded adultery becomes excused. The psychologists, psychiatrists, sociologists and professors have made sin cute and unreal; they say, "It is a different culture, that's all."

Sodom had a different culture too. (I will not go into Sodom's culture, now; I could not do so without blushing before a mixed audience.) But this was their way of looking at things: When a stranger came to their town at night, they said, "Where are the men which came in to thee this night? bring them out unto us, that we may know them" (Genesis 19:5 KJV).

The angels of God smote the place and pulled Lot in and said, "We'll handle these."

Later, fire came down from heaven and burned the whole city of Sodom to ashes.

If the gospel does not change a person, transform them and take the evil out of them, then they do not have the gospel in power. The gospel is a transforming power; otherwise we have merely a name to live but in reality we are dead.

A certain gangster out in California heard about the Billy Graham campaign and decided to go and hear him. He showed an interest and even talked to the evangelist. Finally, Mr Graham said to him, "If you give your heart to Jesus Christ, you're going to have to do some changing."

The gangster said, "Am I going to have to give up my Jewish religion?"

Mr Graham replied, "You're going to have to become a Christian."

Well, the man pounded out angrily and never went back. He was not willing to give up his religion for Christ.

We now use an excuse; we say, "Well, tell him no – he doesn't have to change anything; he just has to believe on Christ." Thank God, Billy did not do that. He lost a friend and made an enemy, but he kept his own garment clean in this matter.

A man who has really been born anew lives by a new moral code. He does not go to the psychiatrists, the psychologists, the sociologists or the anthropologists and say, "What do you think of the Sermon on the Mount?"

A Greek philosopher gathered around him a group of young men who believed in that philosopher completely. If he said something, it was so. No further discussion was needed. I never knew a philosopher I trusted that much, but I know a Man I trust that much.

"And the angel answered and said unto her, The Holy Ghost shall come upon thee, and the power of the Highest shall overshadow thee: therefore also that holy thing which shall be born of thee shall be called the Son of God" (Luke 1:35 KJV). I can trust him.

Therefore, my moral code is Christ. Jesus said, "You've heard it said so-and-so, but *I* say unto you ... " He said it and that is our moral code. I do not need to go to a philosopher to find out what Schopenhauer thought about it. I do not care what that old scoundrel thought about it. I do not even care what Plato thought about it. Jesus Christ is the one who saves me, if I am saved. He is the one who transforms me. He is the one who stands with bleeding hands, pleading for me. He is the one who shall raise me from the dead. He is the one who shall stand as my advocate above, as my Savior by the throne of love.

The man who is a Christian does not ask someone else, "Did Jesus Christ say that? Well, then, I'm going to obey it." In all this, he acts upon his faith and lives it, not only in his public life, but in his total life – in private as well as in public. At any cost to himself, he will follow Jesus Christ and carry his cross if he is truly born anew. He will follow Christ regardless of the cost in property or the cost in pain or even in life itself.

There is a danger of our falling short here. There are millions who have a name to live, but they are dead. You think I mean the liberals. No, liberals do not have any name to live. They do not pretend to live. They say, "I don't believe in that stuff. I believe you should just be good, fan the fires within you and love your brother; be nice and you will be all right."

I am not talking about liberals; I am talking about people who are supposed to be Christians, who have received the gospel but received it in word only. It has never come in power because it has none of the fruits of power about it.

Nobody thinks this could be true of themself. It will pay us to do some heart searching in this terrible hour. The only safe thing to do is to surrender to the power of the gospel. Surrender to the words of Jesus Christ for your life, your home, your business, your property, your private life, your personal life, your secret life. Surrender it and do not let any area of your life as big as a postage stamp belong to the devil. Give everything to Jesus Christ, everything.

You say, "It'll cost me my job." All right, God will find another job for you. "I have been young, and now am old; yet have I not seen the righteous forsaken, nor his seed begging bread" (Psalm 37:25 KJV).

Someone will also say, "But I'll get stuck in jail if I follow the Lord." All right, go to jail, and sing as Paul and Silas did.

"I'll lose property." All right, lose your property. It is better to live in a rented house, and a poor one at that, than have a mansion on the avenue with questions, uncertainties and moral spots all over it. It is far better to come clean and get right, pay up and confess up, than go along and cover up, having a name to live and being dead.

Remember, the Word can come without power and leave us with a name to live, but dead. The Word can also come with power, to transform, change and regenerate us, make the old things new and make us examples to the world. Which do you want?

And can it be?

And can it be that I should gain
An interest in the Savior's blood?
Died he for me, who caused his pain?
For me, who him to death pursued?
Amazing love! How can it be
That thou, my God, shouldst die for me?

'Tis mystery all! The Immortal dies!
Who can explore his strange design?
In vain the first born seraph tries
To sound the depths of love divine!
'Tis mercy all! Let earth adore,
Let angel minds inquire no more.

He left his Father's throne above,
So free, so infinite his grace;
Emptied himself of all but love,
And bled for Adam's helpless race.
'Tis mercy all, immense and free!
For, O my God, it found out me!

Long my imprisoned Spirit lay
Fast bound in sin and nature's night;
Thine eye diffused a quickening ray,
I woke, the dungeon flamed with light;
My chains fell off, my heart was free;
I rose, went forth and followed thee.

No condemnation now I dread;
Jesus, and all in him, is mine!
Alive in him, my living head,
And clothed in righteousness divine,
Bold I approach the eternal throne,
And claim the crown, through Christ, my own.

Charles Wesley (1707–1788)

CHAPTER 7

The Nature of God's Kingdom: Not in Words Only

1 Corinthians 4:1–21

Paul embraced his authority as chief apostle from the Lord for several reasons, the main one being to receive and shape church truth. Paul received the revelation from God. Jesus said:

> *I have yet many things to say unto you, but ye cannot bear them now. Howbeit when he, the Spirit of truth, is come, he will guide you into all truth: for he shall not speak of himself; but whatsoever he shall hear, that shall he speak: and he will show you things to come.*

> **John 16:12–13 KJV**

That Spirit entered Paul when Ananias prayed for him; he was filled with that same Holy Spirit. Then he was appointed by the Lord to set up a system and quality for the church. Perhaps most important of all, Paul was to show by example the Christian way. As he said: "I sent unto you Timotheus, who is my beloved son, and faithful in the Lord, who shall bring you into remembrance of my ways which be in Christ."

When he wrote this epistle, Paul's authority was being

challenged by schismatic men who were teaching that Paul was not a real apostle, alleging that he had never seen the Lord. Their argument was that the other apostles had walked with Jesus but this man Paul had never walked with him; he came along after Jesus had died and risen. They overlooked the fact that Paul, as "one born out of due time", had received a vision of Jesus. These schismatics and dividers of the church had to repudiate Paul's authority in order to establish their own. As far as Paul was personally concerned, their criticism did not matter. He said, "... with me it is a very small thing that I should be judged of you, or of man's judgment: yea, I judge not mine own self" (1 Corinthians 4:3 KJV).

Paul was saying, "I do not even judge my own self. I'm in the hands of God." But he knew that, if he was going to have any influence, he had to establish his authority. So he sent Timothy to straighten the critics out, and finally warned them, "I told you before, and foretell you, as if I were present, the second time; and being absent now I write to them which heretofore have sinned, and to all other, that, if I come again, I will not spare" (2 Corinthians 13:2 KJV). Paul refused to listen to these schismatics and puffed-up fellows. Isn't it strange, that there is nothing new under the sun?

So many of us imagine that we are originals, but there is nobody original except Adam. If you find "puffer-uppers" – men who are puffed up – now, recall that Paul wrote, "Now some are puffed up, as though I would not come to you. But I will come to you shortly, if the Lord will, and will know, not the speech of them which are puffed up, but the power" (1 Corinthians 4:1819 KJV).

Here is what I particularly want to emphasize. The kingdom of God does not lie in words. I am among the few, in this day, trying to tell the church this. There are a few that see it, but not very many see what they saw back then. A person sees the Word by the form of truth. Words are only the outward image of truth and can never be the inward essence. Words are incidental.

Suppose I were to say, "Everybody that can speak Swedish, bring your Swedish New Testament next Sunday to church, and everybody that speaks German, bring yours. Any Norwegian, bring yours" – we would have the Bible in half a dozen different languages. I would say, "Now, read that fourth chapter of 1 Corinthians." It would be quite a revelation to hear that the words were only incidental; it was the meaning that mattered. Somewhere in the middle of the words, there is a spiritual meaning. Six different people embodied that meaning in six different sets of words, and those were not alike or only occasionally alike. We ought to remember that.

The kingdom of God is not in words. Words are only incidental and can never be fundamental. When evangelicals ceased to emphasize fundamental meanings, and began emphasizing fundamental words, and shifted from meanings to words and from power to words, evangelicalism began to go downhill.

There is an essence of truth, and it may follow the form of words as the kernel of an English walnut follows the conformation and configuration of the shell. But the shell is not the kernel, and the kernel is not the shell; and so, while the truth follows the form of words, it sometimes deserts it. There is great heresy in holding the form to be the essence, and putting the kingdom of God in words, thinking that if we have the words right, we will have the whole thing; and if we can get a better set of words, we will have more truth. This is not necessarily true.

Words deceive even good, honest Christian people. We feel that, if we mumble words, there is a certain safety to be found. Some believe there is power to frighten off Satan in mumbling certain words. Would you tell me, please, why the devil should be afraid of words? The devil, who is the very essence of ancient created wisdom and had the perfection of beauty and the fullness of wisdom, and whose power lay in his shrewdness and intellectual prowess – can you tell me how that devil should suddenly become so foolish as to be afraid of a word or a motion or a symbol?

To keep the devil away, I may put a chain around my neck or make a motion with my fingers in front of my face. I wonder what a man without any arms would do, an amputee, if the devil came after him and he could not make a sign of the cross? But the devil is not afraid of words or symbols. You can surround yourself with religious symbols – Protestant, Catholic or Jewish – and you have not helped yourself in the slightest, because the devil is not afraid of a symbol. He knows better.

Did you ever see a little child that is afraid of a false face? Put a mask on, and the child runs away yelling. If the child did that at 16 years of age, you would be ashamed of them. As soon as we grow up, we know that false faces do not mean anything, and words do not mean anything as words. Still, we imagine that if we say certain words, we will have power to bring good. If we say certain other words, we have power to fend off the devil. We imagine there is safety in mumbling words. If we fail to mumble the words, we are in for it! But if we remember to mumble the words, we will be all right. That is just paganism under another form. At best, it is a religious veneer.

The Greeks loved oratory; they loved fine language and produced a lot of fine literature. Paul said, "You Greeks love fine words", but he also said, "For I determined not to know any thing among you, save Jesus Christ, and him crucified. And I was with you in weakness, and in fear, and in much trembling. And my speech and my preaching was not with enticing words of man's wisdom, but in demonstration of the Spirit and of power: That your faith should not stand in the wisdom of men, but in the power of God" (1 Corinthians 2:2–5 KJV).

We ought to throw off this fear of words, as being superstitious and not Christian at all. You may feel a little bit mentally naked when you throw all this off. When you strip superstition away from a person, they feel terribly naked for a moment but, until we strip off our superstition, the Lord cannot put on us a cloak of truth.

The kingdom of God lies in power; its essence is in power. The gospel is not the statement that "Christ died for our sins according to the Scriptures." The gospel is the statement that Christ died for our sins according to the Scriptures plus the Holy Spirit in that statement, giving it meaning and power. Just the statement itself will never do it.

Some churches drill their young people from childhood in the catechism and teach them doctrine, so that they are positively instructed in the words of the truth.

Somehow, they strangely fail to get them through to the new birth. A whole generation of so-called Christians are drilled in the catechism and know doctrine; they can recite the gospels as well as the law; still, they never manage to break through to the new birth. They never come through that shining wonder of inward renewal. The reason is that they are taught that the power lies in the words, and that if they get the words, they are all right.

Paul alleged that the kingdom of God does not lie in words at all. The kingdom of God lies in the power that indwells those words; we cannot have the power without the words, but we can have words without the power. And many people do have the words without the power. So we need to understand that the power of the Spirit operating through the Word – *that* is the gospel. It is the statement that Christ died for our sins according to the Scriptures, that he rose again, that he was seen of many, and that he is at the right hand of God and will forgive those that believe on him. That is the gospel in its shell, but the power must lie in there or there will be no life in it.

Paul appealed away from man-given authority. He appealed away from talk, however eloquent, and even from his own position. Instead he appealed directly to the power of the risen Lord, manifested through the Spirit. Paul said, "I want you to know this power, and I sent Timothy to try to straighten you out and to remind you that it's the power of God that talks, not a man's mouth."

Paul's appeal was to the power of the risen Christ. If the evangelical church and the people who compose it are not living in a constant miracle, they are not Christians at all, because the Christian life is a miracle. It is what the ark of Noah was in the days of the flood. The ark was completely separated from the flood and yet floated upon it. This is how Jesus was when he walked among men – right in the middle of them, yet separate from sinners. There operates within the true body of Christ a continual energizing of the spirit that makes a continual miracle. The Christian is not somebody who believes only; a Christian is somebody who has believed in power.

The working of this power is a moral power. It has power to expose sin to the sinner's heart. Nobody will ever be truly saved until they know they are a sinner, and nobody will ever know they are a sinner by simply being threatened, warned or told. You can go to a man and say, "You are a sinner. You swear and lie; you are wrong; you are evil." He will grin, shake his head and say, "I know. I shouldn't do those things, but I guess we're all human." You have not convinced him. You can read Plato, Aristotle, Herbert Spencer and all the rest of the books of ethics, and show him he is dead wrong, but he still will never know what it is to be a lost sinner. You can threaten him that if he does not look out and does not straighten out his ways, an atom bomb will get him, but you still have not convinced him. You have not told him anything he did not know.

However, "when the Holy Ghost is come," said Jesus, "he will convict the world of sin, and of righteousness, and of judgment" (John 16:8 KJV). When Peter preached at Pentecost, the Scripture says the listeners were pricked in their hearts and cried out, and said, "What shall we do to be saved?"

That word, "pricked", is a word stronger and deeper than the word "pierced" in the passage where the soldier pierced the heart of Jesus with a spear. The words of Peter in the Holy Spirit penetrated like a spear, but even more deeply than the spear that penetrated the heart of Jesus on the cross and brought forth water and blood.

The Holy Spirit is not something that we can argue about or Somebody about whom we can say, "Well, you believe your way and I'll believe mine." The Holy Spirit is an absolute necessity in the church. There is a power in the Spirit which is able to expose sin and to revolutionize, convert and create holy men and women. Nothing else can do it. Words will not do it. Instructions will not do it. Line upon line and precept upon precept will not do it; it takes power to do it.

This power is a persuasive power to convince, persuade and break down resistance. It is also a worship power, creating reverence and ecstasy.

If we were to put statues all around the church, and have candles burning and beautiful, Italian-made colored-glass windows, and pictures of shepherds and altars and all of that, and if I were to come in wearing a long black robe, you would have a certain sense of reverence. But true reverence is not created by beautiful windows (although I like to see them), nor by symbols; reverence is astonished awe that comes to the human heart when God is seen. I can imitate holy tones and try to be as religious and ecclesiastical as I can, and still, when it is all over, the feeling I get is merely psychological, or ecstatic at best.

But when the Holy Spirit came upon the early church, the onlookers dared not join themselves to them. The sinners fell on their faces and said, "God is in this place of truth." So there is a power to bring reverence, to excite ecstasy and to bring worship; and it lies in the Word when it is given in power.

In addition, the power of the Holy Spirit brings the magnetic power to draw us to Christ, exalting him above all else and above all others. We must demand more than correct doctrine, though we dare not have less than correct doctrine. We must demand more than right living, though we dare not have less than right living. We must demand more than a friendly atmosphere, though we dare not have less than a friendly atmosphere. We must demand that the Word of God be preached in power and that we hear it in power.

In 1 Thessalonians Paul said to his readers, "For our gospel came not unto you in word only, but also in power, and in the Holy Ghost, and in much assurance; as ye know what manner of men we were among you for your sake" (1 Thessalonians 1:5 KJV). When the Spirit of God, through the Word, is preached in power and is heard in power, then the objectives of God are wrought. Unholy men are made holy, sins are forgiven, and the work of redemption is done.

The way to obtain this is through prayer, faith and surrender; this is the old-fashioned way and I know none other. As God's people, we have every scriptural right to demand that we hear the Word in power. If we do not hear the Word in power, we have a right to rise up and ask why. If we hear nothing but teaching, nothing but

111

instruction, with no evidence of God in it; if the preacher cannot say, "I appeal to God" to say whether the teaching is true or not, then we have a right to demand that somebody preach that can.

On the other hand, everyone who stands in a pulpit to preach has a right to expect that the congregation believe in power and are so close to God, so surrendered, so full of faith and so prayerful that the Word of God can work in power.

It is amazing how religious, social atmospheres can permeate a church, so that it is hard to tell which is of the Holy Spirit and which is simply nice, social contact. I believe both ought to be in the church and I believe they both can be. When the early church met and broke bread, they fulfilled both their spiritual communion and their social fellowship. Therefore, there is no reason why the two cannot be fused. There is no reason why the warm cordiality of social fellowship cannot be made incandescent with the indwelling Holy Spirit, so that when we meet and shake hands, sing and pray and talk, we do both together. We have social fellowship plus the mighty union and communion of the Holy Spirit.

Let us be very careful that it is both, not one only. To try to destroy or prevent social contact and social fellowship is to grieve the Spirit, because the Spirit made us for each other. He meant that there should be social fellowship and friendliness together. He meant that we should break bread, not only formally in a church but also when we meet. He meant that we should know each other by our first names and have our social fellowships. He meant this, and any church that has tried to destroy this succeeds only in creating a lopsided and fanatical type of church.

However, let us be very careful not to mistake the one for the other. So let us have a friendly church, let us have a morally right church and let us have a church where correct doctrine is taught. But let us also have a church that any preacher can go to and say, when he goes away, "I know the entrance I had unto you, that I could preach unto you, not in words only, but also in power, in the Holy Ghost and in much assurance, because you are the kind of people that could take it." This is most important, for the kingdom of God lies not in words, but in power.

LOVE DIVINE, ALL LOVES EXCELLING

Love divine, all loves excelling,
Joy of heaven, to earth come down,
Fix in us thy humble dwelling,
All thy faithful mercies crown!
Jesus, thou art all compassion,
Pure, unbounded love thou art;
Visit us with thy salvation,
Enter every trembling heart.

Breathe, O breathe thy loving Spirit
Into every troubled breast!
Let us all in thee inherit,
Let us find the promised rest;
Take away the love of sinning;
Alpha and Omega be;

113

End of faith, as its beginning,
Set our hearts at liberty.

Come, almighty to deliver,
Let us all thy life receive;
Suddenly return, and never,
Never more thy temples leave.
Thee we would be always blessing,
Serve thee as thy hosts above;
Pray, and praise thee without ceasing,
Glory in thy perfect love.

Finish, then, thy new creation;
Pure and spotless let us be;
Let us see thy great salvation
Perfectly restored in thee;
Changed from glory into glory,
Till in heaven we take our place,
Till we cast our crowns before thee,
Lost in wonder, love, and praise.

Charles Wesley (1707–1788)

CHAPTER 8

The Characteristics of a Carnal Christian

1 Corinthians 3:1

Some people think of a spiritual Christian as a rather tragic, anemic, mousey, soft walking, soft-spoken, gentle and harmless person who walks about with a permanent smile and cannot be roused to any kind of spiritual indignation. I do not find this to be the scriptural definition of spirituality. If so, then Jesus Christ, John the Baptist, and John and Peter could not be said to be spiritual men.

The carnal Christian is regenerated but is carnal and spiritually imperfect, retarded in his development. It is possible to be spiritually retarded, just as it is possible to be retarded in our physical, spiritual and mental development, having the characteristic of a baby. Paul uses the word "babe" here: "And I, brethren, could not speak unto you as unto spiritual, but as unto carnal, even as unto babes in Christ" (1 Corinthians 3:1 KJV), which is an anonymous description, such as the phrase "babes in Christ".

The church of Christ includes at least four classes of people.

First, there are the average church people who come all the time but are never converted. When they come, they seem to enjoy it and they have friends among the

Christian people but they themselves have never passed from death unto life. That is one class.

Second, there is another class: those who are trained to be Christians but are not. They appear to be Christians because they have learned the language, and they are able to perform certain things, giving everybody the impression that they are in fact Christians. Usually, they can be found in charge of all of the activities of the local church.

Third, there are true Christians, but they are carnal. They have never developed into mature, functioning Christians. They are where they were when they were saved.

Then, thankfully, there are those who are true Christians, and they are spiritual. Unfortunately, they seem to be in the minority in most churches.

I want to zero in on the carnal Christians. They seem to form the largest group in the contemporary church. They drain the church of power and influence while contradicting clear Bible teaching. Paul said those characteristics were unspiritual, they were carnal, so when those characteristics are present in a Christian, we find an unspiritual Christian. The best way to understand this is to compare the carnal Christian with a baby.

Everyone is familiar with the delightful antics of babies. Personally, I love babies. In our home, we have had our share – and then some – of these delightful creatures. Allow me to note their characteristics.

Babies are self-centered

The baby has a little world all of its own and has no idea there is any other world but its own. It is a self-centered little thing; everything else; its mother, father, brothers and sisters, all revolve around that little, central sun. All others are but bodies and are insignificant to the baby. It defines its world by "me", "mine" and other such phrases.

This is Paul's concept of a carnal Christian: somebody who is self-centered, living a self-centered Christian life. They are born again, certainly, but living so that everything revolves around them. The only meaning others have is in relation to the baby's needs.

Babies are unduly affected by their feelings

A baby's quality of life revolves around its feelings. The slightest change in its feelings will have great repercussions on life in general. Every baby demands a perfect environment, which simply means one that complements his or her feelings. One moment, it is a happy little baby and the next moment, it is crying as though its world has ended. Evidence always gives way to feelings and emotions.

Normally, we draw a conclusion based upon evidence, rather than going along with feelings. However, carnal Christians tend to live by their feelings.

For example, they must have what they call a good atmosphere in the church; only then have they had a good time. If there is not a good atmosphere, they do not have a good time. If this continues, they will look for a place more conducive to having a good time. They are more or less victims and fools of their environment.

A baby is a victim of its environment, a willing victim, because it hollers like a banshee when anything goes wrong. Although its finger may stop hurting, a baby cries long after it has forgotten why it started, because it is unduly affected by its fears. Or else it is too hilarious and too humorous for no reason in the world.

I discovered this with our little granddaughter, Judith. If you put your nose down on her nose and mumble, she mumbles, and will go into hilarious laughter, and we have a good time together! I wonder what is so funny about that? I do not know what is so funny about it, but she thinks it is one of the richest pieces of humor that have ever come to her little, year-old circle of interest or attention. She and I do that now; that is our fun together. I do not think it is funny, but it is humorous to see her go wild about it.

Babies are either cast down for no reason or hilarious for no reason. They are victims of their feelings and their senses, because they are carnal in faith. This also is the characteristic of a carnal Christian. They are carnal – too easily lifted up and too easily cast down. They cry when there is nothing to cry about and laugh when nothing is funny. After a while, a Christian should learn better.

Babies rest in everything external

A baby has no inward life at all. Psychologists say that a baby is born without a mind and as it grows, its mind develops. I do not know about that, but I do know they are born with a certain capacity, but without anything in their little minds. Give a baby a brightly colored rattle and it will entertain itself for hours. As it gets older, the capacity develops, but it has no inward life. Babies rest completely in the external.

This also is characteristic of a carnal Christian. They live too much in visible religion and go by things on the outside. They enjoy colored lights and strange or pretty sounds, and certain garments or uniforms, or certain decorations – anything that feeds their childish mind by calling it out from the outside, from the internal to the external.

We may be just as sure of this as we live, that just in proportion as we are affected by external circumstances, we are carnal. For Jesus said, "… the hour cometh, and now is, when the true worshippers shall worship the Father in spirit and in truth: for the Father seeketh such to worship him" (John 4:23 KJV). There is no way that the external can worship the Father perfectly. The carnal Christian cannot worship without religious rattles and toys; otherwise, they get bored and lose interest.

For the mature Christian, any unlovely place is suitable for worship if the heart is right and the Spirit dwells within us. Worship and communion with God can be real and unaffected; the tranquility remains the same because the spiritual Christian does not rest in the external.

Babies have a complete absence of purpose

A baby sees a ball and wants it. They do not know what the ball is or what they will do with it once they get it, but they want that red ball that lies just beyond their reach. They have not yet learned to crawl so they must howl for it and, when they get it, they are let down because they have no purpose. They did not want it for any purpose so, once they had it, no purpose would be fulfilled. That, of course, is characteristic of babies.

Sweet as they are (and I would not want them different – they are the loveliest things on earth), babies nevertheless lack purpose in life. But when a child gets a little older and starts crawling, when it begins to say things or to put things away, it is starting to work towards something. By the time it reaches its teen years, it will have a life purpose worked out for itself.

Just as a baby has no purpose at all, I find that the carnal Christian has no purpose, either. They live for the next lesson. They want to know where the good preacher is going to be, and off they go to hear him. They want to know where the fine choir is going to sing, then they go and sit down and tickle their carnality by listening to the finest choir they can find. Or they want to know where the biggest crowd is assembled, and they get a charge out of the crowd. There is no purpose there; they never went aside and got on his knees and said, "God, why was I ever born? Why have I been redeemed? What is this all about?" Their life is totally without purpose.

Babies spend their time playing with trifles

A baby is the most unproductive creature on the planet. We love them, but all they do is create work for their parents. They live a life of play and trifles altogether.

Everything they do has to be turned into play. A baby will nurse on its bottle for a while, then toss it out on the floor and laugh hilariously when it sees the milk spill and the top come down on the rug. Everything has to be turned into play for babies.

I want to be nice about this; I am trying hard to be nice but, if we are realistic at all, we will have to say that the modern generation of Christians is living for play and trifles.

I have a folder from a certain Bible conference, advertising a trip out on top of the bounding billows on a luxury liner. The participants were to have everything their hearts could wish. There are pictures of beautiful palm trees and all the rest, like Florida or California. It was to be a strictly chaperoned, luxury liner, with a chaplain on board who would give talks on Romans, just before the shuffleboard game every morning, to give a religious flavor. According to the brochure, the purpose of this was to promote interest in missions. I did not get the connection. To me it would be more missions-wise, instead of spending money on the cruise, for everyone to give that money to missions.

Another group advertises, "Walk today where Jesus walked yesterday." I liked what a certain evangelist wrote: "Yes, but not with the same purpose."

We want to play and have no hesitation advertising our Bible conferences as religious playgrounds, which proves how carnal we are. We live a life of play and trifles. In order to get many Christians interested in Bible study or missions, it must be camouflaged as play to make it more palatable. A carnal Christian must be tricked into studying the Bible by having it made out to be something that is fun.

Babies are petulant, fretful and quarrelsome

Mothers often tell others how their baby is a nice little angel. The mother means well, but that little baby is not a perfect little angel. It is a normal baby; it kicks and makes ugly sounds when it is only two months old. This petulance and fretfulness is strictly an immature reaction because it is the temptation to blame secondary causes. All babies do it and eventually grow out of that stage.

I can always tell a carnal Christian because they blame secondary causes. When they lose their job, they blame their boss, instead of blaming their sheer ineptitude and inability to come through. And some Christian women say that if they had a good spiritual husband, they would be a better Christian. They know they would not be; they just think they would because they would have fewer reasons to be a poor Christian. As long as we give ourselves nothing genuine to think about, we can think we are better than we are. However, we use the excuse of a grouchy husband that will not shave on Sunday morning and sits around in a T-shirt – we say he is our trouble. No, he is not our trouble. He could be our sanctification if we knew how to use him. And if we knew how to use opposition, we could turn it into a help.

A carnal Christian always blames secondary causes. I never knew a baby that took the blame for anything, for it is always somebody else that is at fault.

Babies live on a restricted and limited diet

A baby lives on a diet of milk and strained vegetables. Indeed, that is a picture of a baby – someone not yet able to digest solid food. Everything it consumes has to be processed to accommodate the delicate digestive system.

A carnal Christian marks they Bible at tender little passages and skips over those rough passages that tear us apart, bring us down, discipline us and chasten us. The carnal Christian is not able to handle the "meat of the Word". Everything must be predigested and given in measured doses so as not to offend their delicate digestive system. The apostle Paul addressed this in Hebrews 5:13–14: "For every one that useth milk is unskilful in the word of righteousness: for he is a babe. But strong meat belongeth to them that are of full age, even those who by reason of use have their senses exercised to discern both good and evil."

A carnal Christian and a baby share common characteristics. A self-centered little person affected by their senses, resting in externals, without any purpose, loving to play and having no serious purposes in life, living on a simple diet – well, there we have a picture of a baby. Nature takes care of a baby pretty soon. Nature begins to shift the baby out from the center – not altogether, of course, for self-centeredness is part of sin. Still, a child begins to get some interest away from itself and learns to stand up and defy its senses. It learns to reason, instead of living by its senses, learns to live for the character within rather than for external things, learns to have a purpose in life, even if it is only to be an actor or a ball player or something else. But the child develops a purpose; nature takes care of that for most of us as we mature. However, as regards spiritual things, that is another matter dealing with fallen nature.

In spiritual things, what shall we do? How can a carnal Christian develop into a spiritual Christian? For a baby, it is a natural development, but this is not so for a Christian.

I know of no single experience that would instantly transform a carnal Christian into a spiritual one. I would like to be able to say that I do. I wish I could say that I positively know how you can come to the Lord, meet certain conditions, cease to be carnal and become a spiritual Christian. It is simply not that way. We must let the Spirit teach us, discipline us, mature us, grow big within us. We must let God walk within us, and learn by trial and error, by prayer and repentance, by fears and trials of heart, or else we have carnality. Then, we must believe in the power of God to fill us with his Spirit and begin to work with the soul; this leads us away from self-centeredness and leads us to love the whole world.

The old saints used to sing, "I'll Leave the World Alone". They believed that Christians ought to leave the world alone, that we should pray for the world, but leave it and follow Christ in surrender and self-denial.

Then, we have to tell God that we expect him to teach us to live above our feelings and our senses. This is a difficult discipline in the Christian life.

Three young men from a religious institution in the Chicago area came to see me in my study. They were having a tough time of it. One was in trouble because when he got down on his knees he did not have any desire to pray. This troubled them and they thought because I was an older Christian I never had any difficulty like that.

In essence, I told them that there are times when I have had to force myself to pray at all and, for a little while, there is not any peace in it. Their faces began to shine. One of them said, "Oh, what a relief! I thought I was backsliding because I had troubles like that."

There are times when we will not always feel spiritual, but we must pray through it. We have our fight down here and must learn not to trust feelings. When you get up in the morning feeling that you wish you had not, and in the evening you wished even more ardently that you had not, do not let that get you down. A baby will worry about that and holler for Mother, but a grown-up Christian says, "Well, this was not my day."

No doubt, Paul had his days when things were not going right. So we keep our faith in God and Christ, and know that no matter how we feel, it is all right anyhow. A spiritual Christian stops resting in externals.

Mature Christians know why they are here. They know the purpose God had put into their lives when he created them. I find myself sometimes confused in my circumstance, and self-contradictory. If I did not know my Bible, know God, and if I were not able to point back to certain markers where the stones were set up at the Jordan (because this is God's blessing), I could easily blow my blessed ministerial top. But I do not do it because I know that there are certain purposes I am fulfilling. So, I have a purpose.

Carnal Christians have to have their religion turned into play. They drink a while, throw the bottle on the floor, laugh about nothing and get blue about nothing, which is carnality. Spiritual Christians have a life of labor and look upon the world, not as a playground, but as a battleground.

As regards their "diet", real Christians use their whole Bible. This will make some of you mad, but if you are living on your morning daily devotions taken out of a book that somebody compiled, I warn you that is pabulum. Read the entire Bible. Read it all. I do not say these other things are harmful; I just say that, if you have that and nothing else, you are not matured in your Christian life. Read all the Bible; read the "begats" and "begottens"; read it all. A real Christian ought to be able to take a sure, rounded diet.

Now, that is a spiritual Christian, in contrast with the carnal Christian. Not the mouse people imagine, but rather a person who has learned, who has grown up in God, and is mature and growing in the Spirit. That is the spiritual Christian. So let us ask God to make us mature Christians and to grow in grace and in the knowledge of our Lord Jesus Christ.

HIMSELF

Once it was the blessing,
Now it is the Lord;
Once it was the feeling,
Now it is his Word.
Once his gifts I wanted,
Now the Giver own;
Once I sought for healing,
Now himself alone.

Once 'twas painful trying,
Now 'tis perfect trust;
Once a half salvation,
Now the uttermost.
Once 'twas ceaseless holding,
Now he holds me fast;
Once 'twas constant drifting,
Now my anchor's cast.

Once 'twas busy planning,
Now 'tis trustful prayer;
Once 'twas anxious caring,
Now he has the care.
Once 'twas what I wanted,
Now what Jesus says;
Once 'twas constant asking,
Now 'tis ceaseless praise.

Once it was my working,
His it hence shall be;
Once I tried to use him,
Now he uses me.
Once 'twas power I wanted,
Now the Mighty One;
Once for self I labored,
Now for him alone.

Once I hoped in Jesus,
Now I know he's mine;
Once my lamps were dying,
Now they brightly shine.

Once for death I waited,
Now his coming hail;
And my hopes are anchored,
Safe within the veil.

A. B. Simpson (1843–1919)

CHAPTER 9

The Remnant: An Alarming Doctrine

Romans 9:27

I want to articulate a doctrine in the Bible that is very troubling and alarming. I am very much afraid that the Bible is a more alarming book than we know. I love this hymn:

Thy Word is like a garden, Lord,
With flowers bright and fair;
Thy Word is like a deep, deep mine;
And jewels rich and rare
Are hidden in its mighty depths
For every searcher there.

Thy Word is like a starry host:
A thousand rays of light
Are seen to guide the traveler,
And make his pathway bright.
Thy Word is like an armory,
Where soldiers may repair,
And find, for life's long battle day,
All needful weapons there.

All of that is true and I like this song. I enjoy singing it and I enjoy hearing it. However, I am a little bit afraid that

that is the attitude we take towards Scripture – that it is a beautiful jewel to wear around our neck or on our finger, or a fragrant corsage to wear on some dressed-up occasion when the stars shine. Scripture is all of that. But it is something more than that and, in our simple elegance, I am afraid we are not letting the Word of God mean to us what it ought to mean.

Listen to what Isaiah said: "Esaias also crieth concerning Israel, Though the number of the children of Israel be as the sand of the sea, a remnant shall be saved" (Romans 9:27 KJV).

Whatever the educators may say, whatever the current religious vogue may be, here is a doctrine clearly taught in the Scripture, which cultists have misread and have wrested to their own destruction. For every cultist says, "I'm the remnant", and every group that meets says, "We are the people." But I refuse to reject the doctrine just because somebody else has wrested the doctrine to their own destruction. I have neither starry hopes for you to admire, nor any posies for you to smell, but a terrible doctrine that hurts and bothers and makes me sorrow in spirit. It is the doctrine of the remnant.

What is that doctrine? It is simply this: that in our blind, fallen, sinful world of mankind, at any given time, the vast, overwhelming majority is lost. And by "lost" I do not mean they have missed their way or come short of the mark or are less than they wanted to be or have failed to fulfill their dream. By "lost" I mean alienated from God and an enemy to him, without pardon, without life and without hope.

What does this word "remnant" mean? It means a small

fragment, a surviving trace. It means something that yet remains when the larger body is somewhere else.

The text from Romans deals with Israel but it sets forth clearly the doctrine as applying to the entire human race as well as to the church. This was true among the nations before Abraham, it was true of Israel after Abraham and it is true of the church since Pentecost.

I am alarmed because it has been true since Pentecost that a vast number of people who call themselves Christians – the overwhelming majority – are nominal and that only a remnant is saved.

Look at some examples in the Bible. Jesus said, "And as it was in the days of Noe, so shall it be also in the days of the Son of man" (Luke 17:26 KJV).

According to the Scripture, "Noah found grace in the eyes of the Lord". There were seven other members of his family who were also saved from the flood (Jesus refers to Noah as the eighth person). I do not know what the population was, but I know at the time of the flood there were eight persons saved out of a whole population. And I know that it is written, "As it was in the days of Noe, so shall it be also in the days of the Son of man."

Somebody says, "Mr Tozer, you're taking it too seriously. Don't you remember when Elijah felt the way you feel and Elijah said, 'O Lord, I alone am left.' And God said, 'Cheer up, Elijah, I have news for you. Seven thousand are in Israel that have not bowed their knees to Baal nor to his image.'"

That sounds like a lot. Isn't that encouraging, knowing that in Israel 7,000 true Jews did not bow their knees to Baal?

131

Allow me to indulge in a little speculation. Suppose the population of Israel at that time was seven million. I think that is a very conservative count. That would mean that one tenth of one percent had not bowed their knees to Baal, and all the rest had. It would mean one in 1,000. If you were to take at that time 1,000 Jews, 999 of them were secretly bowing the knee to Baal to keep out of trouble and only one man stood boldly.

But suppose for the sake of absolute fairness we cut the population of Israel in half, and say there were only three and a half million. Then it means one in 500. Every time you saw a synagogue or a building with 500 Jews reading the Torah or listening to the chant of the priests, there were 499 secretly following Baal and only one that was saved.

Remember, at Christ's first coming there were only a few that recognized him. We take it for granted, just as Israel did, that when Messiah came they would know it.

They believed just what Samson believed when he went to sleep in the lap of Delilah. He believed that he was well set for life and that, because he had had some experience in religion, there was nothing to worry about. But when he woke up, he found he had been captured; soon his eyes were put out and he was grinding at the mill, and they were making sport of him in the name of a false god. He took himself for granted, which always is a bad and dangerous thing to do.

Either we take ourselves for granted and have a sham peace, or we get disturbed and then pray through and find true peace. Most believers today take themselves for granted and have a false peace. If they did what the Bible taught, they would be bothered and alarmed about themselves; they would go to God with an open Bible and let the Bible cut them to pieces and put them together again, then give them peace. And the peace they would have, after being chopped to pieces by the Holy Spirit and by the sword of the Spirit – *that* peace is a legitimate peace.

There are two kinds of tranquility, do not forget it. Well, maybe there are three kinds now. There's the kind that can be bought in bottles and then there's the kind we get from taking yourself for granted and believing good things about ourselves that are not true. That brings a certain tranquility to the mind.

Then there is the tranquility that comes following a disturbance of the soul that shakes it to its foundation and drives a man or woman to God with an open Bible to cry, "Search me, O God, and know my heart: try me, and know my thoughts" (Psalm 139:23 KJV). Then, when God does that, we have an experience with God that gives us a tranquility grounded upon the Rock. But with most evangelical Christians today, their leaders go outside to bring them tranquility.

The first offer from the Lord is not tranquility at all. The Lord at first offers us deliverance, forgiveness, renewal and making things right; following that, comes tranquility. But we are marketing tranquility now, selling it like soap, and asking our people in the name of John 3:16 to come and get tranquilized. And so we have a tranquilized church that is enjoying herself immensely at banquets, times of fun, coffee clatches and fellowships. She is singing about the Lord, "Thy Word is like a garden, Lord."

I call attention to this only because there is a danger that we make the Word of God into something to give us tranquility. In the wings of churches, the ones that are left open all day in the busy sections of cities, there are people who come in and sit down. They do it, as the poet said, "To invite their souls and call in their thoughts of home and abroad and get still".

Businessmen and advertising men do that; mystics from India and from Burma do that. But it is not necessarily a Christian thing. It is a good thing but it is not enough. We gear our services to tranquilize people and paralyze them, when we ought to be alarmed by this doctrine of the remnant. We ought not to allow ourselves to take ourselves for granted. We ought to be alarmed about it.

Paul was troubled about this and wrote, "But I keep under my body, and bring it into subjection: lest that by any means, when I have preached to others, I myself should be a castaway" (1 Corinthians 9:27 KJV).

I have known preachers that preached a lifetime and ended up as filthy old men, telling dirty stories. It is entirely possible for us to teach Bible school and be on boards, to sing in choirs and take part in church services, and then finally find out we are castaways and have never been of the remnant at all. That is an alarming thing, and I do not apologize for alarming you. I am afraid that we are not alarmed enough. We ought to be disturbed about this, for it is here, summed up in our text, "Though the number of the children of Israel be as the sand of the sea, a remnant shall be saved."

There were a few old friends of God during Jesus'

time, but not many when you think that the population of Jerusalem alone at the time of the Passover was a million. At Pentecost, there were also a million people in that city, and 3,000 were converted. We say, "What a vast harvest that was!" In my opinion, 3,000 out of one million is not a vast harvest.

I wonder if there has ever been a time when there was a vast harvest. I know it was said of John Patton that he went to the New Hebrides and found not a Christian, and that when he left, there was not a heathen. But I have always crossed my fingers when I read that statement because it is not according to the doctrine of the remnant, which is: "Though the number of the religious people should be as the sand of the sea, only a remnant shall be saved." It is not that they could not be saved; it is not that God does not want them to be saved; it is just that they are not saved.

When Christ came, there were shepherds and wise men. We hear about these friends of God, that there were a few of them, and we are glad for them. But the point is that they were typically small, percentage-wise.

Consider also, the second coming of Jesus. He says that at that time, "... because iniquity shall abound, the love of many shall wax cold" (Matthew 24:12 KJV).

It does not say: "the love of many" only, but every student of the Greek will tell us the same thing: there is an article – a positive, definite article – in there: "the". The love of many shall wax cold. Jesus also said, "Nevertheless when the Son of man cometh, will he find faith on the earth?" (Luke 18:8 KJV). He did not say he will not find faith but he said, "...will he find faith on the earth?" So at the second coming of Christ it will be as it was in the days of Noah, when Noah, the eighth person, was saved from the floodwater in the ark, and the rest of the population drowned.

If you still want more support for the doctrine, read church history. A small fragment, a surviving trace, always kept the faith while the others took things for granted.

Do you know what is wrong with us as a church today? We are taking ourselves for granted. We are assuming that which may not be true at all, founded upon wishful hoping and not upon sound Biblical experience. We have not been disturbed enough. We have not allowed God to plow furrows on our backs. We have not dared go before God and have the examination made. We have been afraid of what God will find and we would rather wait and wait. Therefore, we have waited and settled down. There has always been a small fragment or remnant, and they have been in the midst of all the rest. And while a million wish it with their lips, there are always millions who worship with their lips, always.

We do not need to imagine that it is an indication of vast spirituality or any high degree of holiness when we see a church door open and multitudes spew out onto the sidewalk. Follow them home. Follow them and see how they live. That is the way to tell. "Wherefore by their fruits ye shall know them" (Matthew 7:20 KJV).

Ask them to lead in prayer. Announce a prayer meeting and see how they will go. Announce a banquet and see how they will come. In the church of God there is a "stop and go" sign; when it says "go" it's for a banquet; when it says "stop" it's for a prayer meeting. The church of God follows this sign and we smile about it, but it is an alarming thing. I do not want to come before the Lord, having soothed and petted people into some false sense of smug spiritual security.

Read church history and see the fragments that lived in the midst of it all. Read about the Waldensians and the Friends of God and the Brethren of the Common Life and how few of them there were, but how many went to church. It is possible to worship God with our lips and not worship God with our lives. If our life does not worship God, our lips do not worship God either.

I am troubled about so many people singing Handel's *Messiah*, especially during Easter season, without the remotest notion of what it is about. They stand and sing, "Come unto him, come unto him" and they do not know what it means. When Handel wrote it, he said, "When I was through, methought I saw heaven open and all the angels of God gathered." That is how he felt. But you can sing it and enjoy it only as music. You can come, sing hymns in church and enjoy only the dignity of the music as a relief from rock and roll.

Read about the remnant 600 years before Christ was born (Ezekiel 9:1–6 KJV).

We say, "Begin in the Kremlin, O God! Begin in the Kremlin and destroy those godless wretches!"

God said, "Begin at my sanctuary."

We say, "Go down to the corner where men in half-lighted rooms sit and slurp beer! Go down there, O ye with the destroying weapon in your hand!"

God said, "Begin at the steps of my church. Begin at my sanctuary."

We say, "Go to the church, O God, where the pastor denies the Bible and has nothing to preach but poetry!"

God said, "Begin at my sanctuary."

But he also says, "Look out, watch for the mark on the forehead" – that indelible mark. He sent the man clothed in linen, with an inkhorn of indelible ink, and said, "Go mark them, mark them."

"Which ones will I mark? The ones that stand and pray the longest, the ones that give the most to missions?"

"No, no," God said, "that is not the test. Here is the test in a day of corruption: those who sigh and cry for all the abominations that are done in the midst of Jerusalem."

That is all they have to do: sigh and cry. The mark is not for those that succeeded in stopping the abominations. Some things are like a wave of the sea. You can stand before a wave and even Paul himself could not shout it back; it would engulf him. But you do not have to get the mark of the remnant on your forehead, you do not have to succeed and you do not have to be popular. You only have to sigh and cry for the abominations that are taking place in the earth.

I cannot stop people from doing what they are doing, but at least I can grieve because they will not stop. And I am going to do that. I am going to let my tears water the footsteps of those who go astray. When the churches will not come back to New Testament standards and worship the Lord our God in the beauty of holiness, if I cannot make them do it or persuade them to do it in this awful hour of crisis, at least I can weep because they will not come. And I can sigh if I cannot weep.

I do not know what the future holds. I know one thing: rather than betray the sheep of God, rather than lie to them and deceive them and keep them agitated and stirred up with all kinds of popular topics, rather than take my material from magazines, I'll preach the Word to empty seats; I'll sigh and cry for the abomination that is in the earth.

So God says, "Begin at my sanctuary. Then they began at the ancient men which were before the house." It seems to many today that it is young people who are the trouble – these young people that are filled with lust and wild ideas – but the Scripture says to begin with "the ancient men, which are before the house". "These old bearded pillars of the church," says the Holy Spirit, "begin with them."

"And it came to pass, while they were slaying them, and I was left, that I fell upon my face, and cried, and said, Ah Lord GOD! wilt thou destroy all the residue of Israel in thy pouring out of thy fury upon Jerusalem?" (Ezekiel 9:8 KJV).

If the evangelical church, the fundamentalist, believing church will not accept this, then I can at least sigh because they will not, and cry to God because they do not.

FULLY SURRENDERED

Fully surrendered – Lord, I am thine;
Fully surrendered, Savior divine!
Live thou thy life in me;
All fullness dwells in thee;
Not I, but Christ in me,
Christ all in all."

Alfred C. Snead

CHAPTER 10

The Sacred Obligation of Judging

Romans 9:27–28

The question I would like to address is: "Where are those remnants? Where can I find them?"

As soon as we bring this subject up, immediately all of the half-saved and the one-percent saved, the back-sliders, the borderline, the church members, the professors and those who have no witness of the Spirit to their redemption, begin to squirm and quote Scripture. And one Scripture they quote is "Judge not, that ye be not judged" (Matthew 7:1 KJV).

They say, "That man is an old bigot. He judges other people's religion and he judges me. What right has he to judge me? Does not Jesus say, 'Judge not, that ye be not judged'? And does not the Bible say that love 'thinketh no evil'?" (1 Corinthians 13:5 KJV). If that man had love, he would not think evil about anybody. He would accept these, and accept everything done in the name of the Lord and would not say, 'Only a remnant shall be saved.' He would accept the good religious people that go and give of their pennies; he would believe in them. But he's not a man of love, he's not a loving man; he's a severe, harsh man."

I wonder if, when Jesus said, "Judge not", and when Paul said, "Love thinketh no evil", and when Christ said that we should love one another and lay down our lives for each other, if these sayings were intended to end inquiry and silence rebuke? I wonder if Jesus meant, when he said, "Judge not that ye be not judged" that his prophets, his apostles and his preachers were not to go forth and speak truth to the church? I wonder if he meant that they were to go forth like the three monkeys on the whatnot shelf who "see no evil, think no evil, hear no evil" and get a permanent smile on their faces that will never rub off until they die? Are we to believe in everybody who says, "Lord, Lord", and accept them all into the kingdom of God? Are we to forget that the same Holy Spirit who said, "Judge not", through the lips of the Savior, also said "a remnant shall be saved" – a small fragment, a surviving trace.

Do you know what we need in the evangelical church now? We need diagnosis. Do you know what diagnosis is? The word comes from two hard Greek words meaning "to know truth all the way". That is what we need now in the church of Jesus Christ.

Suppose somebody isn't feeling up to par and goes to see his doctor and says, "Doctor, I feel as if I have a mitten in my mouth when I get up in the morning, my head has been bothering me and I don't have any energy. I just don't feel good."

And the doctor says, "All right, stick out your tongue."

The patient looks at the doctor with a puzzled look and says, "What?"

"Put out your tongue."

"I can't understand why you should want me to put out my tongue."

"Well, I've got to know you all the way through. I've got to diagnose you, get to know you."

And the man says, "It's an improper thing to do and I beg your pardon but I won't do it."

"Well," the doctor continues, "how's your appetite?"

"I don't see why that's any of your business," replies the sick man. "Doesn't the Bible say not to ask questions about people and 'Judge not, lest ye be judged'? It says we should love everybody and preach no evil, and not stick our noses into other people's affairs. So why do you ask me about my appetite?"

"Well, how do you sleep?" asks the doctor.

"What difference is it to you how I sleep? I came to you for help – don't you love me?"

"Yes, but I want to know: Do you sleep well at night?"

"That's none of your business, Doctor! Absolutely not. You're a terrible man! Don't you know that the Scriptures say, 'Love everybody, judge nobody, love thinketh no evil and love covers a multitude of faults'? Don't you read the New Testament? Asking me how I sleep... that's none of your business."

"Well, let me take a little bit of your blood."

"My blood?"

"Yes."

"What do you want with my blood?"

"I want to know you; I want to know you through and through."

"I came to you for help. I want encouragement and inspiration. I don't want to give up my blood."

"I can't know you until I see your blood."

"Oh, you are terrible! You're a radical bigot. Why should you want to know about my blood?"

"Well, let me at least take your blood pressure."

"What do you want to know about my blood pressure? It's none of your business. Don't you realize that the Bible says, 'Thou shalt not judge'? If you take my blood pressure, you'll be judging me."

Now, what kind of a crazy business would that be? Satan would hold his belly and laugh in hell. Yet people demand that that is the way the preacher is to feed the congregation.

I want to tell you something. We are beating the drum for revival; we are getting thousands of people to pray into the night for revival. Well, we might as well jump up and down on the altar of Baal, cut ourselves and cry, "Baal, hear us! Baal, hear us!" because we will not submit to diagnosis. We will not let God find out what is wrong with us. We will not let God know us through and through, and we will not listen to the man who tries to find out and minister to our needs.

We go to the preacher for inspiration and encouragement, for confirmation in our backslidden ways. If he's a man who prays half the night for his congregation and would give his life for it, as soon as he opens his mouth we shut him up; we ram this text into his mouth and say, "Don't you dare judge anybody! I'm a Christian and you've got to accept it, otherwise you might be grieving the Holy Spirit." So we shut up the mouth of the man who tries to find out what is wrong and how we can cure it.

If this is true, that I am only to preach love, that I am only to tell you from the book of Ephesians how wonderful you are; if that is true, then all the prophets who spoke since the world began are all wrong – beginning with Enoch, who said,

> *Behold, the Lord cometh with ten thousands of his saints, To execute judgment upon all, and to convince all that are ungodly among them of all their ungodly deeds which they have ungodly committed, and of all their hard speeches which ungodly sinners have spoken against him.*

Jude 1:14–15 KJV

That does not sound much like inspiration and encouragement, and moving onto better things. It sounds to me more like a little diagnosis, like somebody getting into the problem to find out what is wrong.

If I do not dare do the diagnosis and you will not listen to it, then all the prophets were wrong. And Christ was the greatest transgressor of them all – for there was nobody like him that could look you through and make you feel like two cents devaluated. Nobody could do it as well as our Lord Jesus Christ could.

If that is the way it is, that all inquiry must be ended and all rebuke silenced, then the apostles were also great sinners, bigots and heretics. If you do not believe it, read what Paul wrote to the Corinthians, to the Colossians, to the Galatians; read what Peter wrote to the general

Christians scattered abroad, read what Jude wrote about the people that crept into the church. Read what John wrote in his first epistle and all his epistles. Read what James said. Had not these men heard the text, "Judge not, that ye be not judged"? (Matthew 7:1 KJV).

Sure, they had heard that text, but they knew what it meant and these others do not.

Had Paul not heard the text, "Love thinketh no evil" (1 Corinthians 13:5 KJV), when he said, "You lovers of Jewish circumcision are always trying to make Christians with a pair of scissors; well, I wish you'd get clear cut off"? He said, "Get rid of yourself, get out of the church." He was the man who *wrote* this text which says, "Love thinketh no evil" and said that love was the greatest thing in the world and then he told the Galatian false teachers, "Get out of here and cut yourself off."

It is time for diagnosis – to inquire, to search, to get at the blood, to take the blood pressure and find out what is wrong.

I tell you that if we do not, then the mystics were all wrong, the reformers were all wrong; Martin Luther should have been in jail and Charles Finney should have spent a term or two in jail – indeed all of the people who have moved the world for God should all have been in jail.

If that is true, it is also impossible to obey the Scriptures. I dare not exercise moral judgment; I dare not stand up and look at a thing and decide in the light of God's Word whether it is right or wrong. The Lord has given me a commandment, which I cannot obey. "Beware of wolves," he says, "that come in sheep's clothing." Yet the modern theological pussycats say, "Don't judge anybody, but accept everybody at their own face value and be as loving as the Savior was."

All right, then, when the wolf comes along dressed in sheep's clothing, what do I do? I say, "Good morning, Sheepie." And I do not dare allow myself to believe that he is a wolf, even though I see his slobbering fangs! I have to be loving and not judge him. The modern theologians say, "Why, the Lord's using him. Why don't you keep quiet, dear brother? I would be afraid to judge."

Nobody can be quite as effusively affable as these blind folk who are afraid to preach the truth. "Be loving, dear brother," they say, and they paw you with their soft, white hands and call you "dear brother". If I am not supposed to be able to tell a wolf when I see him, then how am I going to keep the wolf out of the fold, which I am supposed to do? Christ said, "Beware of wolves", but if I cannot tell a wolf when I see one, how can I beware of him? How do I beware of that which I do not dare identify? Tell me.

Jesus said, "Wherefore by their fruits ye shall know them" (Matthew 7:20 KJV).

Now, suppose I go out to an old, rundown garden or orchard looking for a sheep-nosed apple, the kind we used to raise out in Pennsylvania. I have been looking around for sheep-nosed apples but all I can find is a crabapple, a thorn apple and a sour, dried-up, degenerative apple, full of worms.

Somebody asks, "What are you doing, Reverend?"

"I'm out here judging fruit. I'm out here looking for fruit."

"But you're not supposed to. Why, the Bible says, 'Judge not' – you are not supposed to judge fruit. Why, I think it's not loving. Doesn't Paul say, 'Love thinketh no evil'? And Jesus says, 'Judge not, that ye be not judged' and 'Love everybody.' Now, that poor crabapple is doing the best he can, and that thorn berry is trying to look like an apple – that's a sheep-nosed apple on the way up, if you would only believe it. Why, the Lord loves the dear thing, so why should you be so hard on it?"

Therefore, I have to go sneaking away. I do not even dare know the difference between a great big, gorgeous, juicy sheep-nosed apple and a crabapple – because if I do, I am judging. So, you cannot obey the Scripture; the Lord has given us truth we cannot obey here. If we cannot exercise moral judgment, criticize and discriminate, then we cannot obey what we have been told to do. John said, "Beloved, believe not every spirit, but try the spirits whether they are of God: because many false prophets are gone out into the world" (1 John 4:1 KJV). Why does he tell us this, if I cannot and dare not try the spirits?

Am I to be afraid to judge when God Almighty sent me to do it? Afraid to distinguish a crabapple from a sheep-nosed apple when God sent me to do it? Am I to be afraid to look at a wolf and say, "You are a wolf", when God said, "Look out for wolves"? Afraid to try the spirits when God said, "Try the spirits whether they are of God"? God is not going to send me out to do something and then damn me for doing it. He is not going to say, "You go out and judge the fruit", and then damn me for judging the fruit.

The Bible says, "Prove all things; hold fast that which

is good" (1 Thessalonians 5:21 KJV). If we cannot exercise moral judgment, then I want to know how we can know good from bad. The scriptural injunction is that if anyone that is called a brother commits fornication, idolatry or some other sin, that we are not to eat bread with them – that is, not have communion with him at the Lord's house. Well, we say nowadays that we dare not do a thing about this. These brothers are dear to the Lord, dear children; they all mean well and therefore we should not say anything about their sins. Paul said, "You had better say something!"

All of our churches have died the same way. They died by getting an infection in them that they could not, and did not, get rid of; soon the infection flared up and destroyed the whole body.

We are where we are because we have silenced the preachers who dared to find out what is wrong with us, who dared to inquire, "Where is the remnant?" or "Is there a remnant?".

So you ask, "What are we to do?" First, let us be aware of something. Let us beware of presumption and self-righteousness. This is the snare of all cults and sectarians, and of the Pharisees. Let us beware of the spirit that says, "I am right; judge yourself by me."

The wonderful thing about a righteous man is that he does not want to talk about it. The wonderful thing about a godly man is that he does not know he is godly. The beautiful thing about a holy man is that he is the only one that does not know it.

As soon as we begin to talk about how holy we are, we are not holy any more – if we ever were. If somebody else says a man is holy, I'll listen, but if he himself gets up and says he is, I close my ears right there; I do not want the decibels to disturb the atoms inside my eardrums because I know he is not telling the truth. A good man does not know he is good; a holy man is not aware that he is holy; the righteous man thinks he is miserable: "Oh, I'm such a poor wretch. I love my Saviour so, and I'm so happy in God, but when I think of myself it makes me sick."

What, then, is the right attitude? The right attitude is to refuse to compare yourself with anybody else. Compare yourself with Jesus.

The person who belongs to the remnant is not asking if they belong to it; they are not inquiring. They are hoping and believing, trusting and seeking and longing, and comparing themself, not with somebody else, but with the Savior. Compare yourself with somebody else and you will be as proud as Lucifer. Compare yourself with Jesus and you will be as humble and meek as Moses.

So the thing to do is not to look for the remnant; the thing to do is to beware of presumption and self-righteousness, and to compare yourself only with Jesus. Then, when you have done that, say, "I am an unprofitable servant."

The point is that you are going to have to come to him in meekness and humility, and not say, "I am holy; stand thou aside." Rather you must say, "Lord God, I trust that, by your grace and the power of the blood of the everlasting covenant, I may gain some little reward. But I'm an unprofitable servant."

It is my opinion – I believe it is more than an opinion; I believe it's insight – that evangelical Christianity, as we know it, is almost as far from God as liberalism is. Its nominal creed is biblical but its orientation is worldly. The modern evangelicals, the Holiness people, the Pentecostal people, we Bible-loving people, we who claim to be evangelical and traditional in our Christian faith – our orientation is towards the big businessmen. You know, Jesus never got along with any of the businessmen in his day and yet we use them as our model.

Our orientation is around the banquet hall.

The evangelical church is orientated around showmanship. I can always tell showmen; I smile to myself and pray that God would wake them up. When I hear a young man leap to the platform, I know where he has been; I know where he has been brought up. He leaps up, just vibrating, and he is a Master of Ceremonies. He learned that from TV. He knows how to do it. He smiles that greasy smile that he puts on with a paddle and he drags that damnable thing into the church. He leaps up and announces the meeting: "And now Mabel Persnickety and Harry Jones will sing! All right, kids!"

I know where he has been, and I sniff no myrrh, no aloes, no cassia, no fragrance of heaven on him. I smell him and I know where he has been. His orientation is TV and movies. But he has a Bible as big as a cedar chest under his arm, and he carries it down the road and says, "I'm preaching a sermon five blocks long, carrying my Bible five blocks." Then he upsets the sermon by arriving at the church acting like a worldling.

We are orientated to play, to respect of persons, to religious bigwigs. We are mousey and timid; if one of these fellows swaggers down the aisle, the little preacher leaps to attention and salutes.

I have a word for you: There is not a person in Chicago high enough in society, or deep enough in debt, or owning enough property, or having enough bank accounts, or able to write a big enough check to shut my little old mouth. Not one. They may be a priest of this, or a cardinal of that, or a bishop of the other. They may be the uncrowned potentate of fundamentalism or the self-appointed without-portfolio ambassador of modern evangelicalism, but I will preach what God wants me to preach.

What can we do? I think the first thing is that we must return to New Testament living. We must get into the Scriptures and discover the level of morality and ethics that are to mark the true believers in Christ. We are to deny ourselves and forsake the world on every level possible, keeping in mind that Christianity and the world do not mix. We cannot have a Christian world; unfortunately, we can have a worldly Christian.

Next, we must resist the magnetism of the majority. For example, we must never allow the majority to overrule the clear teaching of the Word of God. Then, we can return to Jesus Christ as Lord, and throw our loyalty and support on him and all those who follow him.

I WOULD BE LIKE JESUS

Earthly pleasures vainly call me;
I would be like Jesus;
Nothing worldly shall enthrall me;
I would be like Jesus.

He has broken ev'ry fetter,
I would be like Jesus;
That my soul may serve him better,
I would be like Jesus.

All the way from earth to glory,
I would be like Jesus;
Telling o'er and o'er the story,
I would be like Jesus.

That in heaven he may meet me,
I would be like Jesus;
That his words, "Well done", may greet me,
I would be like Jesus.

Chorus
Be like Jesus, this my song,
In the home and in the throng;
Be like Jesus, all day long!
I would be like Jesus.

James Rowe (1865–1933)

CHAPTER 11

The Haunting Memory of Dead Words

In every thought or endeavor at any given time in history, certain words and phrases dominate. They govern the thinking and endeavors of that generation within that field.

It is true in the field of philosophy and it is true in the field of literature, politics and religion. In every generation, every age, every period in history, certain phrases, certain words, certain ideas become lords over the minds of people. And they determine the direction of the endeavor of people in that generation. The power of these words lies in the fact that they embody and express leading ideas.

Do not undervalue the power of an idea. John says, "In the beginning was the Word, and the Word was with God, and the Word was God. The same was in the beginning with God. All things were made by him; and without him was not any thing made that was made" (John 1:1–3 KJV).

When John said, "In the beginning was the Word", he used the word *logos*. This means an "active idea in expression". So in the beginning was an active idea. Everything is made out of that idea, born out of the heart of Jesus Christ, the Son of God.

Everything that is round about us, anywhere where

men live, grew out of an idea or ideas. Let us take a few examples:

Civilization. This idea is so hard to understand that I do not know exactly what civilization is, but it is certainly better than the jungle. It is better to live in the Jefferson Hotel than to live in a mud hut and sleep on the floor. Civilization has its points. It began in the discontented mind of somebody way back yonder, who determined he was going to fix up a little bit and make things better. Our civilization has come out of that idea.

Liberty. There is still some liberty left in this country. All that we have, that we see around us and have enjoyed over the generations, came out of an idea born in the tortured minds of certain men, sometimes even while in prison. These men dreamed high dreams of liberty. Benjamin Franklin, Thomas Jefferson and the rest of the founding fathers embodied those ideas in the constitution of the United States, which William Gladstone said was the mightiest and noblest document ever struck off by the mind of men. It all began with an idea.

Transportation. Somebody somewhere, wearing a leopard skin, discovered the wheel. They discovered that if you took a round thing and put a hole in the middle, you could roll it easily and drag it. So out of that was born the wheel. And out of the wheel came things like automobiles, airplanes and trains.

Communications. Guglielmo Marconi, an Italian inventor, was one of the first to develop a commercial, workable form of radio communication. It is supposed that he sent and received his first radio signal in Italy in 1895.

People then had further ideas that became active and out of these came radio and television.

The Reformation. A man named David, under inspiration of the Holy Spirit said, "Blessed is the man unto whom the LORD imputeth not iniquity, and in whose spirit there is no guile" (Psalms 32:2 KJV). This idea went to sleep for a long time. It came to life again in the heart of the man Paul, and he gave us the books of Romans and Galatians. The idea leaped into the thinking of the early church and then went to sleep again for a long time. It was brought to life once more, in the mind of a man named Martin Luther and the minds of some of his helpers, and the result was the Reformation.

It was out of the tortured heart of a man, Dr A. B. Simpson, that the Christian and Missionary Alliance was born. It had to be an idea before it could be a society. So the whole Christian and Missionary Alliance, with its missionaries all over the world, once lay in the heart of this Canadian man. It was an idea not as big as an acorn, scarcely so big that it could be measured, but it was there.

Ideas are mighty things. Never undervalue them. But there is a catch in this whole business. Ideas, words and phrases have a way of living for only one generation and then dying. However, after they die, they refuse to fade away; they still dominate after they are dead.

In religion, we see this more clearly than in any other field of human endeavor or thinking. God will come along and give to a generation a living idea that is good for that hour, a living truth. This living truth will become clothed, incarnated, in a glimpse of a phrase or a word or half a dozen phrases. This phrase will get itself into a bibliography. It will have books written about it, magazines dedicated to it, preachers going up and down the country preaching it. It will have schools gathering around it; it will become a school of thought in its generation. Because it is a living idea, and it came from the heart of God, it is alive, creative and powerful, and great things are born out of it. Then it will die. It will die in the heart of the people it helped to create, usually the next generation.

After that, the idea will continue to dominate. But in this instance, what we have are the dead phrases and words for an idea that once was living but is so no more. Yet those dead words and phrases continue to determine our doctrine; they determine how the preachers in a particular group will preach, what they will teach in their school, what they will get in their magazines and write in the books that they will sell, and what they will sing in their songs. Nobody recognizes that the word died a generation ago. That word is bandied around by everybody, tossed around, and becomes the catchword and center for great groups of people, even whole denominations. Yet that word died a long time ago and it has no life left in it; it does not do what it set out to do. What it did originally, and to the first one or two generations, it has ceased to do.

And so we continue, for another generation or two, to be dominated by the ghosts of theological words, by zombies of the tomb. We live with dead things that walk like the living; we listen to spectral voices that call out of the tombs of theology, out of the musty, bone-filled tombs where the dead lie. Nobody ever has the courage to challenge this and say, "This thing is dead", and look to God for a live idea. And so we have the great, dead hands of theological phrases choking us. Our lifeblood is being choked out by the continual use of words that once meant something, and still mean something to some people, but do not mean anything to us.

I am going to name only two of these words, both of which are passive words.

1. "Accept": The doctrine of moral passivity

"Accept" was a good word at one time. (Incidentally, in the sense of "accept Jesus", this word does not occur in the Bible.) But there was a time when "accept" was a living idea. This was due to a set of circumstances at that time, spiritual experiences and conditions being what they were in a given generation. Living voices rose and said, "You're not saved by works; you're saved by accepting Christ", and there was life to this idea. Men who had been trying to climb to heaven on Jacob's ladder of good works suddenly discovered that they could accept Christ into their heart and be converted like that. It was a wonderful word in its day.

In the great campaigns of a former generation, "Accept Christ" became the catchword for evangelicalism, fundamentalism, full gospelism and world missions. It contained a mighty truth that has long since died, but the word still stays on. It stays on as a theological specter, producing a generation of Christians, or so-called Christians, that are impenitent in their heart, frivolous in their spirit and worldly in their conduct. We tell people that come to us to be converted, "Accept Jesus"; and they say, "All right, I'll accept Jesus." So they accept Jesus and that is about all there is to it. There is no transformation; no impenitent root of their being is ever cured. There is pride that has never been crucified, a worldliness that they have never been able to deal with, and a frivolity of spirit that is beyond description. A whole generation of people are running around today, victims of this dead theological word, "accept".

To give an illustration of what I mean, there is one place specializing in reaching out to young people in the services and talking to them about the Lord. They have members of staff who are supposed to witness about the Lord Jesus to these young servicemen and women, just before they go overseas.

One day one of their workers, a Baptist preacher, came to me in my study. He threw himself down on a little old davenette and said, "Brother Tozer, I'm in agony. I'm working at such-and-such center. Do you know what the trouble is down there? They will not let me mention repentance. All I dare tell the people going out to die is that they should accept Jesus. The result is that they bow their heads and say, 'Yes, I accept him', get up with a sort of pitiful smile, and shake my hand. Some of them are scared kids, on their way out – and they may not come back – and I don't even dare talk to them about repentance of life or sin, or sorrow for sin. I'm bound only to say, 'Accept Jesus'."

The damage of this will be seen in future generations when the church will be anemic and worldly oriented in all aspects. To "accept" Jesus and not demand a

transformed man or woman will result in actually reject-
ing the Christ of the New Testament.

All over the country, evangelists blaze abroad the message, "Accept Jesus", which has become in our day nothing more than a theological zombie. It is a voice out of the
tomb, which means nothing to this generation.

2. "Receive": The doctrine of spiritual passivity

The outworking of this "receive" doctrine is nothing
short of a tragedy.

When I was a young man, I happened to get into the
company of an elderly woman, God bless her memory.
She did not have too much theology. But she believed
the way to get filled with the Holy Spirit was to get down
on your knees and die out, and open your heart and get
filled with the Holy Spirit. Not having very much theology myself either at the time, thank God, I obeyed. And
the result was an old-fashioned, mighty invasion of my
nature by the Holy Spirit. That is why I cannot preach any
sermon without mentioning the Holy Spirit and the baptism of the Holy Spirit, because I received that baptism.

It was not long, even then, until Christians began to
say, "*Receive* the Holy Spirit." Some hungry-hearted, pen-
sive-looking young person would ask, "How do I receive
the Holy Spirit?" And their teacher would say, "Why,
receive, just receive him. Do you receive him?"

"Yes, I receive him."

The tragedy is that the young person did not receive
him. So we have sent people out by the dozens, even

to the mission fields, who have nothing better than the doctrine of spiritual passivity.

These are dead words, though in another set of circumstances, at another moment, they may again leap to life and become the very words of God for a generation.

These words have been abused and allowed to die; they have died in the house of their friends. The result is that we do not receive and, whatever kind of belief we have, it does not change our life.

I once received a long-distance call from a woman in the city of Boston and she said, "I just finished reading *Divine Conquest*, and my husband and I want to come to Chicago and be filled with the Holy Spirit."

"Well," I said to her, "you don't have to come here to be filled with the Holy Spirit."

She said, "But wait a minute, I don't know anybody in this city that will tell me how to be filled with the Holy Spirit."

I did not know exactly who to tell her to see; I suppose there are people who could have helped her, but couldn't talk too long over a phone. I said, "Sister, I can't have you coming here." She wanted to bring her husband too; both were candidates. I said, "You go and read *Divine Conquest* on your knees, both of you, and keep on reading it until the fire falls."

She said, "Do you think that will work?"

I said, "That'll work all right." I do not know what happened but I trust that is what happened.

Many other words could be illustrated as being dead to this generation of Christians, but these two are destroying the very nature of the church. If something is not done to correct this, the next generation of Christians will suffer from deep spiritual maladies that will keep them from being the testimony to their generation that God fully intends them to be.

WONDERFUL WORDS OF LIFE

Sing them over again to me,
Wonderful words of life;
Let me more of their beauty see,
Wonderful words of life;
Words of life and beauty,
Teach me faith and duty.

Christ, the blessed one, gives to all,
Wonderful words of life;
Sinner, list to the loving call,
Wonderful words of life;
All so freely given,
Wooing us to heaven.

Sweetly echo the gospel call,
Wonderful words of life;
Offer pardon and peace to all,
Wonderful words of life;
Jesus, only Savior,
Sanctify forever.

Our dear Savior will come some day,
Wonderful words of life;
Come to rapture his Bride away,

Wonderful words of life;
Glory, glory, glory,
Shout the wondrous story!

Chorus
Beautiful words, wonderful words,
Wonderful words of life;
Beautiful words, wonderful words,
Wonderful words of life.

Philip P. Bliss (1838–1876)

CHAPTER 12

Some Live Words for Today's Church

Nobody would deny the power of words. In the kingdom, we must be careful that the words before us are live words that are doing what they are intended to do. Despite the fact that many words have died in the house of their friends, there are live words imbued with power from on high. I want to give you some live words – words that are not zombies, not dead things, but living things for the hour.

Purgation

This word occurs in the Bible: "Purge me with hyssop, and I shall be clean: wash me, and I shall be whiter than snow" (Psalms 51:7 KJV). The meaning is that David desired to be purged from his old sins. The word "purgation" is a good word for our day.

What a difference it would be if a soldier on his way out to die was asked, "Private Jones, have you been purged from your sins? Are you clean by blood and fire?" I think you would get under that boy's skin more than if you simply asked, "Will you accept Jesus?"

Of course he will reply, "I will", and bow his head and say, "I accept Jesus" – and nothing will come of it. What a difference it will make to people if we go back to a living, biblical word and say, "Jesus Christ came that he might *cleanse* people."

This is the day of excusing sin instead of purging sin. An entire school of thought has developed justifying sin within the church and trying to prove that sin is perfectly normal, and therefore acceptable. Books are written to justify raising a little bit of hell and still being a good Christian. It is a terrible state of affairs and we need to bring these fiery words back again.

Somebody will say that if we go around telling people they ought to be purged from sin, they will think we are crazy. But we cannot do very much unless we are a little bit fanatical. If we insist upon being proper, we will be as sterile as a mule – and a mule is the most sterile thing I can think of. That is our trouble today: we are sterile because we are proper.

The cults are made up of fanatics and they are out running rings around us. But we would rather be proper and have people say about us, "He's a very well-balanced man; he has his head screwed on properly."

I do not want anybody to tell me I have my head screwed on. Nobody screwed the thing on. I do not care if they do say I am a fanatic, a radical. Well, all right, so was Paul and so was Christ; so was John Wesley and so was A. B. Simpson. So is every man that has ever challenged his generation with ideas born of God and dared throw off ideas that are dead – phrases that do not mean what they once meant and have lost their power.

People use phrases such as "separation" and "the regions beyond", phrases that once embodied a living and breathing idea that motivated the entire church of

Christ. Today they cease to live and breathe, and we propagate and perpetuate the graveclothes of ideas that died. Therefore, "purgation" is a word I recommend to you. Have you been purged from your sins?

Illumination

Nobody expects to be illuminated anymore. I believe, however, in inward illumination. If a person is purged from their sin, there will be an illumination inside them.

We learn from history that the Quakers knew this illumination within. They had a light within. And the old Methodists and some others knew it too. They raised up a generation of people without much education and with few social graces: they picked their teeth with penknives and threw chicken bones to dogs in the governor's palace, as Peter Cartwright did. But they had gone to the place where they received a sudden flash of illumination from above and they knew the inward light.

The very fact that so many questions are being asked these days is a terrible indication that we are not being illuminated. The illuminated man does not ask questions; he answers them. However, in our day, everybody asks questions. People will surround you and begin asking questions about this theological nicety and that doctrinal hair-splitting, and about shades of theological meanings.

There was a generation of plowboys years ago, who got up, stood up in their blue jeans and knew more theology than could be learned in any school.

The man Isaiah said, "In the year that king Uzziah died

I saw also the Lord sitting upon a throne, high and lifted up, and his train filled the temple" (Isaiah 6:1 KJV).

The man Ezekiel said, "Now it came to pass in the thirtieth year, in the fourth month, in the fifth day of the month, as I was among the captives by the river of Chebar, that the heavens were opened, and I saw visions of God" (Ezekiel 1:1 KJV).

What we languish for in this day are a few people, just a few, who do not have to go and check with anybody to see if they are right. We need even one person with an illumination that nobody can know by nature, a flash from heaven that lights up the soul within.

At first, this person will be kicked all around; everybody will be afraid of them. They are too hot to handle. They will say, "Well, I'm afraid the poor person's in for trouble." They will flop around for a while, then finally find themself and make everybody ashamed they thought this person was a little "off". We need illuminated people in these days. I believe in inward illumination.

Renunciation

Jesus said, "If any man will come after me, let him deny himself, and take up his cross, and follow me" (Matthew 16:24 KJV). We live in a day in which renunciation is no longer being taught. We are not supposed to renounce anything to become Christians. We are not told to. We just believe something and accept something passively, in a state of moral inertia, and then we go right back to what we were doing before. There are people in this country making a career of compromising the cross of Christ with the world, until we cannot tell which is which. We are one big compromise.

When a person is converted, they ought to renounce their old life. We are members of a new creation, born from above, sons of the Father, joint heirs with the Son; heaven is our home, hallelujah is our language and we belong to a little company, a minority group, despised and rejected of men.

Instead of that, Christianity has become popular. Evangelicalism has become popular and, consequently, it is dead. I wrote a little essay called, "Removing the Prayer Meetings: A Pagan Religion". I said, in effect, it is pagan praying when evangelicals pray and go right back to the film set and make another movie.

Someone wrote me a very lovely, intelligent letter. He said, "I'm an evangelical. I am a graduate", and he named a certain fine Christian school. He wrote, "Brother Tozer, your editorial sounded to me like evangelical prejudice against movies. Don't you think the time has come for us to rethink movies in the evangelical circles? There are some good movies and we evangelical Christians ought not to go to the bad ones and thus raise the level of the movies. Your approach sounds to me like categorical dogmatism."

I sat down and wrote him a letter: "Dear Brother, Your suggestion that we evangelicals accept the movies is old stuff. The modernists said that 30 years ago and they rethought the movies, with the result that they and the movies are alike now. There's no separation."

Whenever you hear a person pleading for the right to be worldly, they are covering up a basic unbelief in their heart. The person who has been purged and illuminated will renounce the world, leave it and get out of it. If God converts a movie actress, we Christians have a right to demand that she get dressed, walk off the set and never go back. If God converts a gambler, we have a right to demand that he throw down his cards, walk out and pay everybody that he owes, if he can. He should sell every horse and renounce the old bobtail nag.

But "renunciation" is a word we do not use any more.

Immolation

This word means offering ourselves as a lamb on the altar. When the Old Testament priest took a lamb, put it on the altar, strapped it down and cut its throat, that was immolation. Paul talks about it in Romans 12:1: "I beseech you ... that ye present your bodies a living sacrifice, holy, acceptable unto God." It is one of the things of God that Christians have believed in all down the years but, nowadays, it is safety we are looking for instead of a place to die. God's people ought not to be looking for safety or a place to hide but rather a place to die, a place to give themselves as an offering to God.

God's people want to use Jesus as a lifeboat to get out of trouble, as a bridge over the flames. Then they go back and live as they did before and never seek a place to immolate themselves.

Isn't it time people stopped looking for soft spots and cushions to fall on and places to hide? We who claim to be followers of the lowly Nazarene should begin to immolate ourselves and hunt for an altar on which to die, instead of an easy ride.

A few years ago, I had to settle something and I settled it, I think, by the grace of God. I had to settle whether I was going to get old, peter out, get weak and preach in a high voice; or whether I would look for an easy life, make my bed, move off to a little cottage by a lake, play, and live on my retirement. Was I going to be a voice to this generation, come what may? Was I going to hunt for a place to die and ask God for the privilege of speaking God's Word to this generation?

Adoration

We do not hear much about adoration any more; we do not worship God any more. I like to sing the old hymns; I am a fanatic for the old hymns. But I am a fanatic with my eyes open, because I love to sing the things that adore my Maker. The music of the heart is adoration. The music of heaven is adoration. When we get to heaven, we will find that the harpers harping on their harps are just adoring God. They are not playing "Sweet Adeline" or "Huckleberry Hill"; they are adoring God. Likewise, a Spirit-baptized person will be an adorer of God.

I do not want to say we should go back and be what evangelicals were in the old days. That is old technique and I do not like it to copy it. But I discovered the secret, if you can call it that, of their power in their generation. They loved Jesus until they shouted it out for joy. They adored the person of Jesus. They were harpers harping

171

on their harps; some of their poetry was bad and they sang it off key, but they adored God.

I am looking for the fellowship of the burning heart. I claim the Methodist and the Baptist as mine, and I claim everybody that loves Jesus Christ as mine, but I am looking for the fellowship of the burning heart: men and women of all generations everywhere who love the Savior until adoration becomes the new word. They do not need to be entertained and amused because this Christ is everything to them, all in all.

If we become worshipers of God, God will honor us in the hour in which we live. I think we ought to insist that we adore God, and we cannot adore him until we are purged from our sins, until we are illuminated by a fiery baptism, until we renounce the world and all of its deceptions, and then offer ourselves on an altar ready to die. Burn the bridge and give it all up and then there will be born in our hearts adoration – a true adoration, a worship of the Lord Jesus Christ.

We sometimes sing Watts' old hymn:

I'll praise my Maker while I've breath,
And when my voice is lost in death,
Praise shall employ my nobler powers;
My days of praise shall ne'er be past,
While life, and thought, and being last,
Or immortality endures.

Isaac Watts, the man who wrote that, was an Englishman and a Calvinist; he's the one who wrote, "I'll praise my Maker while I've breath". You say, "All right, then, we've got to be Calvinists in order to be adorers and worshipers." Let me tell you some more.

There was an Arminian one time by the name of John Wesley, an out-and-out Arminian. He did not believe any of this Calvinistic trash-talk, as he called it. He said he believed in the Arminian theology. By the time he was 80 years old, he had traveled 25,000 miles on an old, bony horse's back, had established churches and had set England ablaze.

At the end of his life, he was lying down, too weak to even sing anymore; he wanted to die, but he would not die quite yet. He was waiting to go, and he was trying to sing in the meantime.

His friends around him bowed down really close to this old Arminian as he was dying, and they heard a little squeaky voice, singing. When they got down low enough to hear the words, what do you suppose it was? It was the old Calvinist song: *I'll praise my Maker while I've breath/And when my voice is lost in death/Praise shall employ my nobler powers*. Across the theological fence, Isaac Watts and John Wesley reached out and hugged each other tight, and sang together: *I'll praise my Maker while I've breath/And when my voice is lost in death/Praise shall employ my nobler powers*."

I refuse to fight over theories, but I am looking for the fellowship of the burning heart: men and women who are lost in worship, who love God until he is the sweetheart of the soul.

Let us have the courage to stop using words that have lost meaning. Do not say "Amen" every time somebody gets up and shouts a phrase that we have been reared on.

See whether it is dead or alive. Examine it a bit and say, "Wait a minute here now – is this thing living?" If it is alive, shout! If it is not, bury it.

I thank God I escaped from doctrinal hair-splitters and theological niceties. I thank God I was fanatical enough to shut my eyes and jump, and let God take care of what is left.

Let us get some living ideas now. Let us preach again that men and women can be purged by fire and blood, that the Holy Spirit can illuminate them within, that they are called upon to renounce worldliness of every kind and to offer themselves on an altar to die. Then, if the result is not a fiery bush of adoration, I will miss my guess.

Let us be sincere about all this and we will find that our heavenly Father will come to us as in the ancient times. We can know again the fiery flame and bring the burning bush back to religion.

I'LL PRAISE MY MAKER WHILE I'VE BREATH

I'll praise my Maker while I've breath,
And when my voice is lost in death,
Praise shall employ my nobler powers;
My days of praise shall ne'er be past,
While life, and thought, and being last,
Or immortality endures.

Why should I make a man my trust?
Princes must die and turn to dust;
Vain is the help of flesh and blood:

174

Their breath departs, their pomp, and power,
And thoughts, all vanish in an hour,
Nor can they make their promise good.

Happy the man whose hopes rely
On Israel's God: he made the sky,
And earth, and seas, with all their train;
His truth for ever stands secure,
He saves th'oppressed, he feeds the poor,
And none shall find his promise vain.
The Lord has eyes to give the blind;
The Lord supports the sinking mind;
He sends the laboring conscience peace;
He helps the stranger in distress,
The widow, and the fatherless,
And grants the prisoner sweet release.

He loves his saints, he knows them well,
But turns the wicked down to hell;
Thy God, O Zion! ever reigns:
Let every tongue, let every age,
In this exalted work engage;
Praise him in everlasting strains.

I'll praise him while he lends me breath,
And when my voice is lost in death,
Praise shall employ my nobler powers;
My days of praise shall ne'er be past,
While life, and thought, and being last,
Or immortality endures.

Isaac Watts (1674–1748)

CHAPTER 13

God's Way in His Church

John 5:17; Philippians 2:13; 1 Corinthians 12:4–6

In considering how God works in his church, I want to acknowledge my indebtedness to a woman who has been dead 600 years, Lady Julian of Norwich. I discovered her 600 years after she had stopped living and had gone to live in another, better world. The little book she wrote, which I refer to quite often, is called *Revelations of Divine Love*. I will be using some ideas from that little book that will help explain God's way in his church.

Allow me to lay this discussion out in what I will call five spiritual axioms, borrowed from Lady Julian, that show how God works in his church today. The comprehension of this will go a long way in helping us understand what God is doing, not only in the church universal, but also in the individual Christian's life.

Axiom 1: Everything God does is creative and constructive

God does not do evil. Sin is a work of temporary rebellion against God and its explanation is yet concealed. Sin is concealed, that is, the reason for it – how the great God can be working and yet sin can still be in the world – is concealed from us. We do not yet know, because those concealed things are a mystery. People do not like the word "mystery", but it is a good biblical word that we ought to learn to live with. For the world, everything round about us, is shrouded in mystery, in things concealed. Lady Julian comprehended this and wrote, "And I saw not the creature doing but I saw God doing in the creature."

This is exactly what the Bible says, both in the Old Testament and in the New. Remember that whenever the Lord worked through Gideon, it is described this way (in some versions): "God clothed himself with Gideon." He took Gideon, put Gideon on and worked through Gideon, and in Gideon did his mighty works. It was not Gideon doing it, but it was God working in the man Gideon.

When we come to David and Goliath in the Old Testament, we notice the upholding of this principle that God does everything that is constructive. God does it; not people, or man or creature, but God. This is the reason there was no armor for David.

I do not suppose that there would have been a committee or a board anywhere in Israel that would have gone along with David and allowed him to go out, without armor, to meet the great, overgrown Goliath with his mighty sword as big as a weaver's beam. David could not have argued that idea to anybody. He could have argued, pleaded and written, but he could not have gotten anybody that would have allowed him to go out there without armor. Even he, for a little while, put the armor of Saul on. It was too big for him, so he took it off and said it was not his armor. But if he had had to go through a committee or board to get this armor off, he never would have got it off. They would have sent him out there so loaded down with hardware that he could not have moved; of course, Goliath would simply have pushed him over and trampled on him. But David did not go out that way; he had no armor.

Why did God send a man out without any armor against a giant all covered with armor? Because God wanted to say, "God doeth everything." He wanted to show that "... it is God which worketh in you, both to will and to do of his good pleasure" (Philippians 2:13 KJV). Why did he send David out against Goliath when there was such a vast disparity in size and strength? This man Goliath was a huge man, and David was an ordinary-sized man; I am not even sure that he was not a little undersized. Yet God pitted the two against each other. Why? It was so that David might never boast about it anywhere. David never said to one of his wives, if she got a little out of hand, "Do you remember what I did to Goliath?" He knew he had not done it; God had done it.

Then there were the unequal weapons. The man David simply had five smooth stones – little marble-sized pebbles made round by rolling about in the water – and a slingshot. It was not a rubber slingshot such as children use now – rubber had not been invented; it was made out of a leather thong. Can you imagine God sending a young, undersized fellow out without any armor and without proper weapons against a huge, oversized giant of a fellow who had proved his strength? Why, it is preposterous, but God did it because "it is God which worketh in you".

Notice the difficult passage in 1 Corinthians 12:4–6. God tells how the Holy Spirit works in people and through people. God has a work to do and he does it himself, in and through his people, by the gifts of the Spirit. "Now there are diversities of gifts, but the same Spirit. And there are differences of administrations, but the same Lord. And there are diversities of operations, but it is the same God which worketh all in all." The point is that mortal minds cannot think immortal thoughts.

If we could only know this, we would do a lot of crawling at board meetings instead of coming to them assured that we had all the answers. We would be less inclined to answer all questions and instead we would begin meekly to ask them. Mortal minds cannot think immortal thoughts. God has to think immortal thoughts through us; otherwise our thoughts are mortal thoughts. Likewise, mortal men cannot do immortal deeds. That is a total impossibility. God does his eternal works through the hands of men, but it is the work of God *in* us.

Here is something most people do not know and I suppose we will learn it and forget it: God does not give us a reservoir of wisdom and power. If he did, it would very soon become stagnant. In the case of wisdom, according to the way we think about it God comes to a person, pumps them full of wisdom and says, "If you get into any trouble, come and see me, or call me up and pray. But in the meantime, you have a whole cistern full of power and wisdom here. You draw on that wisdom because it is yours." God never does it that way.

God does not give to a person a word of wisdom, and he does not give to a person power, but he *is* power in that person and he *is* the word of wisdom in that person. It is God working in the person. It is not the person working. If we could only remember that. God becomes wisdom to us and he becomes power to us. This explains how Christians may often blunder so.

If we see a tall baseball player, who has played in the big league for twelve years, we say, "He's skillful; he has learned his game. He's got experience." It is the same with anything people do. They learn by experience; they learn how to do things by doing them. But in the kingdom of God, it is completely other than that. A person can be 75 years old and have served God most of their lifetime and yet they can make a critical blunder and be so ignorant and uncouth, because at that point God is not working through them or in them. That person is right back where they were when they started. It is God which worketh in us.

God did not send me out to be a marriage counselor. He sent me out to preach the gospel and, if he gives me a word for somebody, it is his Word and it will help people. But if I think that I, out of my years of experience, can tell people how they ought to live, I am only making a fool out of myself. Unfortunately there is a great deal of this kind of fool-making going on in the church of Christ in the name of Christianity. We forget that we have no wisdom for anybody unless God wants to give us the wisdom at the moment. Jesus said, "But when they deliver you up, take no thought how or what ye shall speak: for it shall be given you in that same hour what ye shall speak" (Matthew 10:19 KJV).

Every created thing, every eternal thing – God does it, God is doing it. Mankind is not doing it. If he were to strip the churches from all mankind is doing and leave only what God has done or is doing, we would trim the average church back down to a nubbin. There would not be enough left to have a decent service. But all of the churches are running on their own steam; they have learned how. They have gone to school to find out how, and people have written books on pastoral psychology and pastoral theology, which means, "How to Run a Church in Ten Easy Lessons". The answer and the result is that we just do not know what we are doing. We count on our reservoir, instead of on our Lord.

If you talk to a Christian Scientist or a Roman Catholic on Wednesday, and you have an amazing success with them and maybe even win one of them to Christ, and then on Friday you try it the same way, you could fall flat on your face. The reason is that God was working in you on Wednesday, but you were looking to what God did on Wednesday, expecting him to work that same way on Friday. Someone may even write a book about it. I have seen books on how to win Roman Catholics and what to say to Christian Scientists and how to answer Jehovah Witnesses. You can answer one of these people on Monday and answer successfully, then try it on Wednesday and the person will put a half nelson on you and throw you to the mat. It takes the Holy Spirit to work in a man. Always keep that in mind.

God does everything and man is doing nothing. It is only God that is working. Remember, it is the eternal Lord who is creating a new generation and a new creation. Just as Adam did not create himself and just as the angels did not create themselves, but rather God created them, in the same way, God is building his church.

People are not building the church. God is building the church. If he is not building his church, we simply have a religious organization.

Axiom 2: God does all in his foreseeing wisdom

All that God is doing, he is doing in his foreseeing wisdom; nothing is done by happenstance or by venture. Everything God does, he does in his foreseeing wisdom. God knows our tomorrow, he knows our day after tomorrow, he knows all about us down the years, and it has all been planned before our time was.

All that is now happening is within the wisdom of God, established before any star was ever created. Long before there was matter, motion or law, God had foreseen it all. Either you believe that or you will be frustrated and miserable all the time. The Bible teaches that God does it all in his foreseeing wisdom. He foresaw it all and he is not just allowing things to happen. The world is not a truck running downhill with the driver having a heart attack at the wheel. No, the world is moving towards a predetermined end, and God Almighty, standing in the shadows, is seeing it go, watching it and guiding it.

The nation of Israel, the nations of the world, Christendom and the true church that he hides in his own heart – God knows where they all are, at all times, through his infinite and perfect wisdom. He is running everything according to plans which he made before Adam every stood upon the earth. Before there was Abraham or David or Isaiah or Paul, before Jesus was born in Bethlehem's manger, God had this all planned.

Do not think of God sitting down with a pencil and working it out, the way you and I would have to do it. God thinks and it is done. He wills and it comes to pass. God does not have to work with a pencil, a slide rule, a compass and a square, the way architects and builders do. No, and he does not fit and follow in a jumble, the way conventions do. He thinks it done, he speaks it done – and it is done because he thinks and speaks. "In the beginning was the Word, and the Word was with God, and the Word was God. The same was in the beginning with God. All things were made by him; and without him was not any thing made that was made" (John 1:1–3 KJV). How was that done? He was the Word; he spoke and it was done.

When Jacob fled from the face of his angry brother and was in the waste-howling wilderness, he saw a ladder standing up on the earth. I still wonder whether Jacob would ever have seen that ladder if he had not been on the run. Had Jacob been back home in good company, staying around the house helping his mother with the dishes, he never would have encountered the ladder.

I would like to suggest one thing. Sin is always wrong and, when we rebel against God, we are going to get ourselves into really serious trouble. But remember another thing, that if you are God's, you belong to him. And if you have learned the art of true repentance, God will turn even your defeat into a victory. Fleeing, Jacob saw a ladder.

Saul of Tarsus was "breathing out threatenings and slaughter" and one day he stood and watched Stephen die. Undeterred, he went away from there and on his way, on the road to Damascus, he saw the Lord high and lifted up and he heard a voice – and he was a converted man. I wonder if Saul would ever have been converted had he been a quiet professor in Gamaliel's university and had simply said, "Well, there is no use getting excited about it, no use getting excited. Everything will work out all right." If he had said that, there would never have been a Paul: the mighty servant of God. But Saul was a man, the root of the matter was in him, and so God observed the man's wrongdoing, turned him around, started him right and then began to work in his life.

Axiom 3: Much that God is doing looks to us like an accident or a mistake

Due to our blindness and ignorance, we do not know why God is doing what he is doing and so we begin to fidget and wonder if God does really know. However, God sees tomorrow; we see only today. God sees both sides and we see only one side. God knows that we do not know and God has all the pieces to the puzzle. You and I have only a few of the pieces.

Imagine our pattern of life: we would like to see it bloom into a beautiful picture where everything is in place, but the pieces are all scattered around and we do not now where they belong; nothing fits. Did you ever try to put a puzzle together? Two pieces look as if they belong together but they do not; still, you try to force them into place. As you force a piece into place, you break an edge off it and you are worse off than you were before.

Likewise, we take the work of God and we try to push

the pieces together. I think a good part of my life has been trying to shove together pieces that do not belong together, and trying to separate pieces that do. This is due to ignorance; we forget that it is God that gives us the wisdom, it is God that works in us and if we would only know this, we would let God do his work through us and in us. That is why I believe in the gifts of the Spirit. I do not think I have done myself any good with the evangelical hierarchy by coming out as I have, but I have always believed that all the gifts of the Spirit ought to be in the church today, just as they were back at Pentecost.

God is working through his people, and whatever God works *lasts*. Whatever God does not work will not last. I do not care how much personality a man has; he cannot do immortal work because he is a mortal man. He cannot think immortal thoughts because he has a mortal mind. But if the Holy Spirit works in him and through him, he giveth to every man severally as he will. It is the same Father working in us, the same Spirit working through us, and God will do his work.

Those accidents that you and I think we are in are not accidents at all. If a man follows the Lord like a reasonable person, he will not find any accidents. He will find God working his life out for him.

If you trust God, he will bring you out of all that way of thinking. You will see that events are not accidents. The accidents I thought were accidents were simply God helping me through when I did not know he was doing it.

Axiom 4: God never changes; he is perfect

God never changes his purpose. "No, never shall he, world without end." This insight does not sound to me as if it had been given 600 years ago but it was. And it is part of truth: the Word of God, the gifts and callings of God, are without repentance.

God never loses heart. I would like to have you know that. Religious people lose heart. I have seen some good, godly people get into an emotional spin and end up so low there was no describing how low they were. But God never gets low because he sees the end from the beginning; to God, everything has already happened. If you knew you had to die tomorrow, you would feel a little low tonight, for a while, and then you would get elated. But God never gets up and then down, and up and then down. This is because, for God, everything has already happened. God is not going around watching dials and looking at gauges, checking if everything is all right and testing to see if you are on the beat. No, God does not have to do that. "God changeth never his purpose, no, never shall he, world without end." He is moving towards a purpose in Christ Jesus that he had before the world began.

When the angels sang over Bethlehem's manger, they were not announcing anything new. It had been known all the way back to the Garden of Eden; indeed it had been known to the heart of God *before* there was Eden, a garden, an Adam or an Eve.

So God changes his mind never. "No, never shall he."

God said to Jonah, "Go and preach in Nineveh." Jonah

bought a ticket to go in another direction. God changes not his mind, "no, never shall he". Therefore, Jonah ended up preaching in Nineveh.

Conditions may seem helpless. A man asked me one time why God did not condense the Bible – all that old, dry history. Do you know what that old, dry history teaches? It teaches that God works providentially through men; that history is the footprints of God. God worked in history in the lives of men like Abel, Noah, Abraham, Lot, and all the rest down to us; that is why we have heard of these men so much. This is the way God works and he has not changed his mind.

Axiom 5: God never lifts his hands off his work

God leads all things to an ordained end. He never lifts his hands off his work. When Michelangelo died, he had a backyard stacked full of partly completed statues. Michelangelo was an Italian and, in addition to having the high, hot Latin temperament, he had a double charge of genius worth five crowns.

Michelangelo would see a piece of rock and start to sculpt it, but he wasn't willing to wait around; he would get disgusted. So he had a whole backyard full of statues that he had started but not finished, because he lost heart and started on something else. He did an amazing amount of work, but there was an equally amazing amount of work he was too impatient to finish. If he could have given it one more day, it might have turned into what he wanted. Instead of that, he threw it out, so people later found his backyard full of half-done pieces of art.

God never lifts his hands off his work, no, never. Now, I believe that; I do not care what happens, I believe it, so when God says, "You do this", it means, "You go do it and I will work through you and I will not be discouraged; you may be discouraged but I will not."

There is an old saying: "The higher up a monkey goes, the more his tail shows." So the devil rises up and starts his attacks. If the devil only knew that if you hit God's people hard enough, they brace themselves! All we have to do is to get after God's people just enough, and we bring out everything that is in them.

When everything is going all right with me, I am one of the laziest, most easygoing people you ever saw in your life. But when things fight against me, I back up a few steps and suddenly say, "Hold on here!" So the very intention of the devil, to drive me back, actually has the opposite effect.

I believe this is true of Christians everywhere. God does not take his hand off his work; he is moving towards a preordained plan and, if we work with him in that plan, Satan's efforts to stop us can only cause us to snap our teeth sharply and say, "In the name of God and in the strength of Jehovah, we are going forth!"

God never takes his hand off his work but has declared a preordained end by the same wisdom of power and love by which he created everything in the first place. You are no accident; do not think you are. God made all things for a preordained purpose and with foreknowledge. When you came into the kingdom, you were not an accident.

Back in the beginning, when there was nothing, God knew all about that and knew what things he would bring with him when he came. He knew when he would come; he knew what he would say. God never lifts his hand off his work. He works by wisdom, power and love. There is no less wisdom, no less power, no less love now than there ever was.

This is hard for us to understand because we cannot see it. We must believe it. Believing is a kind of seeing and, if I believe what God has said, I am seeing in a sort of way. But I am not seeing down on my human level. Always it is our human nature that gets us into trouble.

Years ago, I heard a man preach a sermon. He said, "The Christian has three men inside of him: the old man, the new man and the you-man. That is all there is until he is converted and then he gets the new man." I liked that. There is a human nature, and the human nature gets into so much trouble. Even long after victory has been won over the old man, the 'you-man' just gets you down. That is the part of our nature that gets blue, the part that gets arrogant and carnal. The old man must die in order to live in the power of the new man, and then the new man keeps human nature under some sort of control.

God does everything in his foreseeing wisdom. While much that he does looks like an accident to you and me, this is because we do not know enough. God never changes his plans and never will; he never lifts his hand off his work but goes forward towards the preordained purpose, using even people such as you or me.

Arise, my soul, arise

Arise, my soul arise,
Shake off thy guilty fears.
The bleeding Sacrifice
In my behalf appears.
Before the throne my Surety stands,
Before the throne my Surely stands;
My name is written on his hands.

He ever lives above,
For me to intercede,
His all redeeming love,
His precious blood to plead.
His blood atoned for all our race,
His blood atoned for all our race,
And sprinkles now the throne of grace.

Five bleeding wounds he bears,
Received on Calvary.
They pour effectual prayers,
They strongly plead for me.
"Forgive him, oh, forgive," they cry,
"Forgive him, oh, forgive," they cry,
"Nor let that ransomed sinner die."

The Father hears him pray,
His dear Anointed One;
He cannot turn away
The presence of his Son.
His Spirit answers to the Blood,

His Spirit answers to the Blood,
And tells me I am born of God.

My God is reconciled,
His pard'ning voice I hear.
He owns me for his child;
I can no longer fear.
With confidence I now draw nigh,
With confidence I now draw nigh,
And "Father, Abba, Father" cry.

Charles Wesley (1707–1788)

CHAPTER 14

The Ministry of the Night

Psalm 74:16

Occasionally an uninspired poet will say something nice about the night such as, "How beautiful is night! A dewy freshness fills the silent air" (from "Thalaba", Robert Southey, 1774–1843). I might quote a few others. But our instinct is away from the night and towards the day (I am talking about the physical night and the physical day) because we are made for the day. We are not nocturnal creatures; we are diurnal. We belong to the day. And in the sacred Scriptures, much is made of the idea of day and night. The day symbolizes the kingdom of God, heaven, righteousness and everlasting peace; the night symbolizes the reign of sin, destruction and ultimately hell.

The purest of the non-inspired concepts of God that I have known or ever heard about is that of the Parsees. They were not inspired, of course. They felt after God, if perchance they might find him, and they came up with the religion we now know as the fire worship of the Parsees or Zoroastrians. Their belief is that God is the light, therefore they worship the sun and they keep fire burning on their altars continually.

Without any definition, but following a thousand analogies, the apostle John says, "God is light." In the light of the day, we have a number of things we cannot have in pitch darkness. For instance, we have knowledge.

A person who stands in pitch darkness may be standing within one foot of a cliff over which they might easily stumble to their death, or they might be standing within one foot of their own door and not know it, because it takes light to bring knowledge.

Also in the daylight there comes a perception of the relation of one thing to another that cannot possibly be present in the night. Mankind is a traveler on his way and, for this, he needs there to be light somewhere. Not even the compass will lead us, if we do not have light to see the compass. There must be light because we are travelers and we must go on our way. Now, just as the sun is the lord of the day, giving knowledge, perception and information, so God is the Lord of the kingdom of light. He is the Lord of the kingdom of holiness, justice, wisdom, love and peace.

God calls us into the light. We are thinking about light in a moral sense now. I would say that the simplest and most elementary description of conversion would be that God calls a man from dishonesty into honesty, from moral wickedness into purity, from hate to love, from envy to charity, from lying to truth, and from evil to good; this, as I say, is elementary and certainly not enough. It does not explain enough but it is true nevertheless. And this call of God, from the darkness of wickedness to the light of truth and holiness, is a constant call, always being heard. When the dweller in darkness comes into the light, what a radiance of beauty they see for the first time! What a lifting of the load is this, what a rolling away of fear! What an inward well of comfort there springs up, and a seeing of the sun. That is conversion.

I sometimes think that, after we have been Christians for a long while, we tend to forget what happened when we were converted. We begin to take ourselves for granted as do a couple that has been married a couple of years or so; the radiance of their first day in their new home fades away and they begin to take each other for granted. I think that every once in a while we Christians, just for the sake of giving our own souls a refresher, ought to go over our conversion again and see what did happen then.

The Scripture says that the day belongs to God; it is talking about the moral aspects of things: light, holiness, morality, purity, joy. All these belong to God. But it also says that the night belongs to God and here we come to a different meaning of the word because the word that we see used here is an extension, borrowed from the old word.

When Israel was down in Egypt, they had "the night" all around and about them. Nevertheless, the night was God's night and belonged to God. So they had light in their dwelling. Many of God's children cannot stand the light of the night.

I must explain again that by "the night" I do not mean wickedness. I mean that state of affairs that wickedness has brought to the world, which we must live in the midst of, but which we are no part of. All the evil that is in the world is here; it is darkness to you and me, but we must remember that the sovereign God holds that in his hands. If there were any part of God's world that he did not have control over, there would soon be a rebellion that would shake the throne on high. But God is the sovereign God and the night also is his. Though he has affinity now with the wickedness of the world, he is still in control of the world. The darkness that comes around us is also in his hands and we are in his hands.

There are those of God's children who cannot learn this. They fear the night and they whither in the darkness. They are children only of the day and they have never learned the ministry of the dark night of the soul. God has to leave a light on for them, just as we sometimes leave a light on for a frightened child until it goes to sleep. And God has to keep some people out of trouble because they are not strong enough spiritually ever to know how to deal with trouble; yet, if they do not have trouble, they will not have growth, and so there is a vicious circle. God cannot expose them to the night and yet they cannot grow until they have had the cooling dews of the night.

Others learn to walk in darkness. They do not walk in moral darkness but live in a dark world. As Peter said, we are in a dark place", "holding forth the word of life" (2 Peter 1:19; Philippians 2:16 KJV). In this sense, we are thinking of the better aspects of the night, not moral evil, but the inconveniences, hindrances and tribulations that result from living in a world of night.

The sovereign God forces even the darkness to serve his will and compels the sullen night to discipline his children. You and I never want it to rain. We want the sun to shine continually but, if the sun shone continually, the earth would be baked. It takes the cool rain mingled with the warm sun to produce the vegetation and to bless the flora and the fauna, which God has given to us to enjoy.

In 2 Corinthians, there is a passage very dear to my heart. It says this: "For our light affliction, which is but for a moment, worketh for us a far more exceeding and eternal weight of glory" (2 Corinthians 4:17 KJV). I want you to see the sharp contrast here. There is affliction but it is light; there is glory but it is heavy. There is affliction but it is for a moment; there is glory but it is eternal. If we could keep this in mind, we would not be afraid of the night and we would not always have to have God to put a light on, to keep us from whimpering.

The night has a ministry to you and me. By "the night", I mean our circumstances in a fallen world – the situations we are in now: occasional visitation of sickness, the loss of a loved one, the failure of our hopes, the disappointment we have when people fail us. Along with these, we experience the attacks of the enemy – the devil himself – coming to us. All of these are, in a sense, darkness at work. We are in the midst of it and we cannot escape it. The Scriptures teach this and often the hymns that we sing also teach this.

I am quite astonished how we sing one way and believe another; how we sing one thing and behold another thing to be true. I think we ought to go over our hymns and throw out the ones we have determined not to believe; we would save ourselves some ink and trouble. I believe if a hymn is true, we ought to hold it to be true and, if it is not, we ought to say so. God loves candid people and he has very little to do with conventional things merely for convention's sake.

So, if it is not true that the cross is a beautiful thing to carry, and that joy cometh in the morning after a night of weeping, then we ought to quit quoting it. If it is true, we ought to start believing it.

God occasionally discovers a soul that he can trust. He lets the mysterious signs come to them, the mysterious evidences that they have been chosen out by him. His hand is laid on their shoulder; he has marked them as being different. They are going to be great Christians, great souls. Let us not think for a moment that all people are alike in the world. They are certainly not all alike in the kingdom of Adam. There are ignorant people, educated people, great people, simple people, small people and large people. There are people with many talents, people with few talents, and a few with none. People are not alike in this world and they are not going to be alike in the kingdom of light either. Some men and women in the kingdom of light are slated for greatness in God's kingdom, while some will simply be there, I suppose, to sit on the golden chairs and fill up heaven. I do not know what else they are for.

I have known many of the Lord's people who are going to go to heaven by the grace of God but they have never been much use here, and they probably will not be much account there, unless the Lord has a new way of doing things that he has not revealed in the sacred Scriptures. But there are some that the Lord laid his hand on and they are going to be great in God. I do not mean famous, I mean great in God: they're going to be rich beyond all the dreams of avarice. God employs every means to make the spiritually great. He uses the day with its sun and he uses the night with its darkness. He uses good people with their hope and cheer, and he uses bad people with their persecution. He uses help with its bounty and perhaps uses illness.

I would rather believe the Bible than believe what I find in a book somewhere. In the Bible, I find a man got sick and, when he got sick, he turned unto the Lord. He said, "Before I was afflicted I went astray but, after that, I returned unto the Lord." The churches believed through the centuries that the Lord sometimes chastens his people by letting illness happen to them. You will find that in 1 Corinthians 11, and you will find much else in the Scriptures that would teach the same thing. So every time you get a pain, do not accept the silly modern idea that that pain is the result of your failing the Lord somewhere. The Lord may turn that pain into glory.

When God Almighty turns loose on us the ministry of day and night, of good and bad, of God and the devil, he makes the devil work for us. He harnesses him like the dumb donkey that he is and makes him pull the cart for the saints of God. God has always done it and he is still doing it. When the devil starts out, roaring to seek whom he may devour, God bottles up his roar and makes it work for the kingdom and for the saints of the most high God. The winds that blow and the stars in their courses fight for the men and women God delights to honor.

The ministry of the night is that heartache we have carried around with us and are carrying now. This is the ministry of the night:

The night of suffering

Job had not only bodily pain; he had the worst pain: suspicion and blame. His own wife turned on him and sarcastically told him that he ought to give up. He said to her, "Woman, I came into the world naked and I am going out of the world naked." She disappeared and was never heard of again. But Job still had to endure a lot of pain. God allowed three eloquent friends of his, friends who had eaten at his table, to come and spout poetry to prove that Job had been a hypocrite all the time. If you think that is easy to take, try it sometimes. Job had it to do, for a long time, and Job said, "But he knoweth the way that I take: when he hath tried me, I shall come forth as gold" (Job 23:10 KJV).

The night of sorrow

Jesus was called the "man of sorrow". That is why I cannot think that we happified Christians, who always want to giggle, are true followers of the man of sorrow. Because Christ was "a man of sorrows, and acquainted with grief" (Isaiah 53:3 KJV), those who follow him will have many nights of sorrow.

The night of loss

I think of our old friend Abraham who took the knife when God told him, "Slay thine only son whom thou lovest, even thine only son Isaac." God grabbed his wrist quick enough to stop it. But all the psychological inward pain of it had already taken place when Abraham said to God: "Yes, I will slay my son." Already he had died inside his heart. Already he was a wounded man slowly bleeding to death. But God staunched the wound, healed him and gave him back his son. He also gave him back everything else, blessed him and made his name great. All the nations of the earth have been blessed through him. But Abraham had to know the sudden settling down of the dark night in the midst of day. He had to know it.

The night of failure

I think of that man Jeremiah. I find many men who wander around in the church that are no good, and many men who are the messengers and saints of God that are not wanted. You cannot always tell whether God is blessing a man by how many calls he gets, because many men get calls who, if the truth were known about them, would never be called anywhere, except to a court of law. Other men are God's own saints but are not wanted.

I remember an old Irish preacher by the name of Robert J. Cunningham, a dear old friend of mine. He always said he was between 25 and 80 years of age, which is all he would tell me; I never knew how old he was. He was one of those men so thin he could not get any thinner and so dry that even his breath did not have any moisture in it, but he was a saint. He would look up at the ceiling and preach to his congregation. They criticized him for praying too much. He said one time, "If it's the only criticism my friends have against me that I pray too much, why it's all right, it's not too bad." He was something of a failure. Nobody called him and said, "Brother Cunningham, come and preach to 500 ministers." Nobody ever said that to him, because he would go and stand up there, look at the ceiling and talk in a dry way. But God was on that man. He was a saint; he walked with God and "was not, for God took him".

Failure is sometimes an evidence of the hand of God upon us. We Christians can afford to fail because Jesus afforded to fail. He died out there on the cross and it looked as if it was a battered, tragic, stupid end of a man who meant well but did not know how to handle himself. On the third day, God raised him from the dead, set him at his own right hand, made him to be head over all things in the church, and put all things under his feet, whether they be principalities, powers or dominions. And yet he died an apparent failure. But only "apparently", for he was a roaring success before three worlds and in this hour, and will be in all the worlds to come. Failure is sometimes "the night".

What did people think of John the Baptist? They said it would have been better if he had never been born. What a failure, what a hopeless wretch he was. I heard somebody say that, when John the Baptist died, somebody on earth said, "Oh, John the Baptist is dead", but somebody in heaven said, "Oh, here comes John the Baptist!" It is all there in our viewpoint; it is all a matter of the way we look at it.

The night of coldness or staleness

I wrote a little editorial entitled "How to Keep from Going Stale". I believe this staleness comes to all the Lord's children, even the best of his children; they get rather dull and cold.

King David had his cold spells and he blamed them on

God. He went to God, and said, "God, you did this. Now bless me and bring me out of it." He did not go off somewhere and try to blame it on his wife but said, "O God, you've turned away from me; bless me now", And the Lord heard his prayer and restored him again to warmth.

Do you ever have those cold periods that you cannot seem to do anything with? Some of you have never had warm periods long enough to know the difference – a person who has never been warm will never find out when they get cold. But for you that have had your long, warm spell, you know there have also been times that were cold spells.

I've got up many a morning and, if I went on my feelings, I'd have lain back down, literally – and not only lain back down but flattened out, given up and quit planning ever to get up again! But we do not work and we do not live according to our feelings. When the time comes for us to pay our taxes, we do not pay them if we feel good, and not pay them if we feel bad. We pay them, period. And when it comes time for us to go to work, we do not say to our wife, "I'm feeling low this morning." We get up and go to work. We walk by faith, we do what we have to do and know we ought to do, and we pay no attention to our coldness or warmness. I admit, though, that it is very nice to be warm.

The night of penitence

Isaiah said that he was undone, that he was a man of unclean lips. We walk by faith and oftentimes a glimpse into our own hearts will so disconcert us and grieve us that we can have no present joy. I find it possible to walk around without any joy. I find it possible to live in the heart of God without any joy for a little while.

By means of suffering and sorrow, loss, failure, cold spells, penitence and tribulation, God makes that which is outward, inward. He perfects the Garden eastward in the souls of each of his children.

Lady Julian said this:

> *For the tender love our dear Lord hath to all that shall be saved, he comforteth readily and sweetly, signifying to us it is true that sin is the cause of all of this pain, but all shall be well and all manner of things shall be well; for the redeemed of the Lord, all shall be well.*

**Julian of Norwich, *Revelations of Divine Love*
(c. 1342–c. 1413)**

The sooner we learn to appreciate the ministry of the night, the sooner we will lose all apprehensions associated with the night.

ALL MUST BE WELL

Through the love of God our Savior,
All will be well;
Free and changeless is his favor,
All is well;
Precious is the blood that healed us,
Perfect is the grace that sealed us,
Strong the hand stretched forth to shield us,
All must be well.

Though we pass through tribulation,
All will be well;
Ours is such a full salvation,
All is well;
Happy still in God confiding,
Fruitful if in Christ abiding,
Steadfast through the Spirit's guiding,
All must be well.

We expect a bright tomorrow,
All will be well;
Faith can sing through days of sorrow,
All is well;
On our Father's love relying,
Jesus every need supplying,
Yes, in living or in dying,
All must be well.

Mary Bowley Peters (1813–1856)

CHAPTER 15

How to Know When a Thing is from God

1 Thessalonians 5:21; 1 John 4:1

I want to share a little spiritual treasure that God gave to me some years back that enables us to tell whether a doctrine is from him or not; whether a blessing we receiving or an emotional experience we may have, or a miracle we may think we see, or anything else, is of God or not.

Some Christians, of course, cannot profit by this for the simple reason that they are static. They have had no new experiences and they are not going to have any if they can help it. They have no crises, no epochs, no advances. They never circle and fly higher. They are satisfied to beat their wings fast and buzz around low. They will not go up there where there is any danger. They can nod and wish it were over, but this little treasure is for us who are seekers after God, who are troubled and concerned about our spiritual lives.

Some people are troubled. They are troubled in their spiritual lives and they read the Bible but that does not seem to help them. They do not seem to be able to find themselves. Because they are troubled, they are ready to listen to anyone – and that is one danger. I do not like to see anybody too willing to accept things. I like to have them do what the Bereans did: examine the Scriptures to see if these things be so.

Some people are eager and seeking some new thing. On the radio, you hear people lecturing, talking and giving messages. This is all right – radio is a good medium of communication. But we have to use our head and our heart, and we have to find out what this person is really talking about. The fact that they get up there, talks fast and sounds pious does not mean one thing in the world. The devil can come as an angel of light, so you have to learn how to know an "angel of light" from an angel of God. You have to learn to know pseudo-truth from truth.

There are those who are willing to take up a new doctrine and seek new experiences if somebody else comes along and demonstrates they have had one. And there are always those who are easily moved by miracles. I have never been that way. I have seen God do some miracles, but I have never been much convinced by miracles. If they will not believe Moses, the prophets, the apostles and our Lord, they will not believe even if a man rose from the dead. Miracles are secondary proofs of anything; yet miracles move some people tremendously and, if somebody can come along and do a miracle, such people will just believe anything.

I want to give you a rule, to help you along this line. The rule is this: Whatever doctrine you begin to get interested in, whatever new religious fad comes your way, whatever religious experience you may seem to be having or have had; check it. You must dare to check it. In fact, you are under orders to check it. And you check it by asking seven questions : How does this affect my attitude towards, and my relationship with, the following:

1. God

Suppose a new doctrine has come my way from some fellow who perspires and talks sumptuously. All right now, he has got his doctrine. What does that doctrine do for God? Does it make God great or small? Does it make God necessary or less necessary? Does it put God where he belongs, does it bring glory to him and does it humble me? Does it show me how little I am and how great God is? Or does it obscure God and draw a veil across the face of God?

Whatever makes God *less* – less important, less wonderful, less glorious or less mighty – is not of God. The whole purpose of God in redemption, in sending the Scripture in the first place and redeeming man, is that God might be glorified among men. The glory of God is the health of the universe. Wherever God is not glorified, that part of the universe is sick. Hell is sick because God is not glorified there. Heaven is abounding in glorious health because God is glorified there. Earth is halfway in between – both sick and well – because only some glorify God and the rest do not. The glory of God is the health of the universe, and the sound of the anthems of praise to God Almighty is the music of the spheres. Therefore any doctrine, any phase or emphasis of doctrine, any experience that I may seem to have, any miracle that I may seem to have seen, if it does not make God big and keep him big and make God indispensable and wonderful, then put it away. Stand and say, "I'll have nothing to do with anything that diminishes God."

2. Christ

Christ is who he is and what he is, and he is indispensable. He is, and always will be, necessary to the point where I must have him. Any teaching, any experience, any fellowship, any activity that makes Christ less necessary to me cannot be of God.

Suppose you have gone to the altar, you have prayed, you have been blessed, and you have heard teachings or emphases given there. The fact that Dr Bounds said something does not make it true. The fact that I have said something does not make it true. The fact that your Bible teachers have said something does not make it true. We can be mistaken. You have to test us, as well as everybody else, and search the Scriptures.

Has our teaching made Christ more wonderful to you? Is Jesus Christ bigger, grander, sweeter and more indispensably beautiful now in your life than he was before? If he is, you have every good reason to believe you have been hearing from God. If he is less glorious and you have become attached to man, then the teaching you have had is bad, or at least it has been given in a bad way. Jesus Christ is absolutely necessary. He is the divine imperative. He is the One without whom we cannot live. We must have him and we must be in him and he in us. If the teaching is from God, your dependence on God and your dependence upon Christ will increase, and Christ will become sweeter and more wonderful all the time.

I do not say he will become sweeter as the days go by. We sing that song and I do not believe it half the time I hear it. The same old deacon will come to church and, every second Sunday morning for 20 years, he will sing "Sweeter as the Years Go By". Yet he is the same sour, sulky, stubborn old person he was before, only he is a little older, that is all, a little more wrinkled. He is just the same mean old Christian that he was 20 years ago. Yet you try to tell me that Jesus is sweeter as the years go by. Well, that man is not moving along with the years, so let us not sing it if we do not mean it. I would rather sit quietly and never croak an "Amen" than to lie to God and the people. But, if Jesus is more glorious every day, there is no harm in saying so and I believe in coming out and saying so.

I believe we ought to practice again boosting our preachers a little bit. Some Christians have sat and looked at their young pastor with cold, level eyes for the last two or three years and are beginning to pray that the Lord will move him. If you had boosted him a little with an occasional friendly "Amen", he might have been a better preacher. He *would* have been a better preacher.

A congregation can take a young fellow just out of seminary and before he knows it he is preaching over his own head. He is doing better than he thought he could do. Why? Because he has been boosted from the congregation.

The sermon tasters will kill any preacher. Maybe the young fellow that comes to be pastor at your church isn't as deep as you wish, but if *you* were as deep as you ought to be you would put up with him for a while; you would pray him through and love him. If you can find one little squeak to appreciate, go tell him so. He will go home feeling good and say, "If that old brother believes I can preach, then my sermons are all right. I thank you, Lord, that I'm improving a little." You could help the man.

Jesus Christ our Lord is indispensable, He is pre-eminent above all, and any experience, any interpretation of Scripture that does not make him big and great and wonderful, is not of God. For God wants to make his Son glorious and the Son wants to make the Father glorious and the Holy Spirit wants to make the Father and the Son glorious. So if an archangel with a wingspread of 40 feet and shining like a neon sign were to come down here and tell me that he has just seen a miracle and wants me to come, I would want chapter and verse. I would want to know he was from God. I will not run after any will-o'-the-wisp.

Of course, I bother many people. They wonder why I am not all worked up about them when they come steaming in. I am not going to be worked up over someone with breath in their nostrils. Here is my book, the Bible. Here are my two knees and I am still able to bend them – and when I get so old and rheumatic that I can't bend them, I can stand up and pray. God Almighty hears his people pray and I have a line open to him. When people tell me that the Lord told them to tell me something, I say, "My line is open to God – why didn't he tell me?" I reject what they say unless it obviously makes God wonderful and makes Jesus Christ beautiful. Then I'll give it an ear, but that doesn't happen very often.

3. The Scriptures

Does this new experience, new interpretation, new preacher or new emphasis make the Scriptures more or less precious to me?

A woman came to me and said, "Mr. Tozer, I'd like to ask you a question. I'm troubled."

I said, "What is your trouble?"

She told me, "Our pastor has gone forward in the things of God and he's gone so fast that he tells us God's given him new revelations that are not in the Scriptures. And he wants us to divest our minds of all that we've learned and follow him, and that we'll be sinning if we don't follow him."

I told her in a nice, scholarly way to tell him to go get lost and that she should go back to the Word of God. No person will ever be able to persuade me to follow them unless they follow the Scriptures. Here is the Book: "To the law and to the testimony" (Isaiah 8:20 KJV). If they speak not according to the law it is because there is no truth in them. "The prophet that hath a dream, let him tell a dream; and he that hath the word, let him speak my word faithfully" (Jeremiah 23:28 KJV). We can always check with the Word.

If this new experience does not make us read the Word more, it is not of God. If it does not make us meditate on the truth more, it is not of God. I do not care how good we feel. If we feel so good we feel brand new, as the Camp Meeting song used to have it, we are still not being blessed of God.

Some might ask, "Is it possible to have an emotional

experience that is not of God?" I should say so. It is entirely possible to get emotional experiences that are not of God. But I believe that true experiences carry an emotional overtone and for that reason I have no objection whatever to emotions. I believe the Lord's people ought to be the happiest and most radiant people in the world and I believe they ought not to hesitate to speak right out and say "Amen" when they feel like it. If they don't feel like it – if it is just a habit – it is just so much dry wood. So we need to examine how these experiences affect my attitude towards the Scriptures.

4. Myself

Whatever comes from God diminishes myself, glorifies God and makes me less and less self-confident. Whatever comes from God humbles me. Whatever comes from God makes the flesh intolerable. But if it comes from the flesh, it puffs me up and makes me feel superior; it makes me look down on other Christians.

Did you ever meet those Christians with their nose elevated at a 45-degree angle from the level field? They smile down from their imperial heights and say, "You do not understand me; just pray about it", and they go away looking like Saint Francis. But all they had was a bad case of pride. It was just pride grown bad, grown cancerous. No, if it is of God, it always humbles us. If it is of God, it makes us appreciate our fellow Christians more. It makes us appreciate the humblest, poorest Christian in the whole congregation and makes us love that Christian.

Self puffs us up and makes us look down on other

people; it makes us feel full of pity for them and smile down on them. Never put yourself on a pedestal. "In me … dwelleth no good thing" (Romans 718 KJV). I do not care who you are, or how many degrees you have; I do not care for anything that you might say or have justly said about you. Any experience that is of God, any doctrine that is of God, certainly humbles my flesh and brings me down to a lowly place before him; it makes him great and makes me little.

5. Other Christians

Do these experiences or these new doctrines or emphases make other Christians more dear to me or less dear to me? Am I drawn to them or is it the opposite? Whatever brings separation in spirit from others of God's children cannot possibly be of God.

You might think that I do not believe in separation. Yes, I do believe in separation. If your pastor is teaching that the Bible is not the Word of God, that Christ is not the Son of God, that the Scriptures are not to be trusted, that they are only partly true, that the new birth is an old-fashioned idea, that the blood does not cleanse, I say the thing for you to do is separate yourself from that pastor. I would not give one dime to support a lazy preacher who reads books written by liberals and then tries to preach them to the congregation. I would not give them a Lincoln penny, not even a dull, old one. But if the preacher loves God, I am going to have fellowship with them.

God will let a movement die and throw it on the fire if it does not keep close to the blood, close to the truth and close to God. If a movement does not keep Christ in it and keep right and keep morally and doctrinally sound, he will let that movement die – unless we keep it alive by prayer, heart searching, good preaching and walking with God. So do not ever think for a minute that there are Christians inferior to you because they do not belong to your group.

Other Christians are dear to me. I am a "catholic " – do you know what that means? That means a "universal" Christian, somebody that believes in the whole church of Christ. I am that. I am not Roman Catholic but I am a catholic, that is, I believe in the universal church of Christ. All of his children are my brothers and sisters.

They that love the heavenly Father love all of his children. I love them all. I love the ladies with their black hats and I love the men with beards: I love the people who wear those uniforms that look like the postman delivering mail and I love the Salvation Army. I love all the Lord's people *if* they are the Lord's people. I will not go along with the liberals and modernists, the God deniers or Christ deniers. I cannot go along with them, no matter if they call themselves Christian.

So ask yourself: Does this new experience make me love all God's people? If it does, it is very likely to be of God. If it makes you feel superior to them or drives a wedge between you and them, chances are it that is not of God.

6. The world

Does this experience or this new interpretation of Scripture excuse worldliness? Does it reason that, because different people have different ideas of worldliness, we cannot be sure about what is worldly or not ?

If it claims that worldliness is just an old-fashioned idea of being separate from the world, it is not of God. The truth will tend to separate us from the world and the world's ways and the world's values. I think it is a lamentable and grievous thing that the average rank-and-file young person in America thinks that to be a movie star would be to reach the final pinnacle of all possible happiness and perfection. I think that is lamentable. Why should a young person choose the lowest order of humanity and follow that as an example?

Some female movie stars have beautiful curves and lovely shapes, but they have themselves photographed half-clad, day and night before the camera, to feed the carnal, vicious lusts of men and women. Then our lovely sweet girls look upon them starry-eyed; if only they could just have their autograph, just touch them!

I saw one of these creations on a train one time. I will not give her name, but she was eating in the dinner car across from me; a woman said she was her secretary, and somebody else pointed and said, "That is So-and-so." She looked just like anybody else. I have sisters that look just as good as she did. She looked quite ordinary. I then went back to my Pullman car after watching her eat. I opened the newspaper, and my eyes fell upon an advertisement regarding this same woman, showing her going to the town where they were going to put on one of her big deals. Boy, she looked as if she had had a permanent wave given her by the angel Gabriel and had borrowed her glamorous clothing from Gabriel. She looked as if she had dropped right plump out of heaven, the dust not off her wings yet. Out in the dinner car she was just a homely little woman, sitting there looking like any other homely-looking woman, but when they got through with her she looked like somebody else.

Then we want our young people to imitate these phonies. If we want to imitate somebody, we should imitate Susanne Wesley; she had 17 children and John Wesley was the last one. You can thank God on your knees, for the rest of your life, that John Wesley was ever born. Thank God, if you will, for Monica, the mother of Augustine. Thank God for good women. Pick missionaries and pastors' wives and saints in your church back home: simple-hearted, glorious people with hearts that are wondrous and full of grace. Pick them and imitate them, and you will thank God all through eternity you picked the right models. Do not pick the wrong model.

Any doctrine that makes the world your friend is not your friend. Any doctrine that makes it easy for you to hobnob with the world and the world's ways, to accept the world's values and do things the way the world does, is not of God; it cannot possibly be.

7. Sin

If this new interpretation of Scripture, new experience or new teaching is of God, it will make sin intolerable. The closer I come to God, the more intolerable sin becomes. Yet I have heard people who have had spiritual experiences say, "Sin is not sin to me any more. God has made me holy inside; I cannot sin. Therefore I can do these things that would be sin if other people did them." The devil certainly crawled up inside that person before they ever started teaching that doctrine. Sin is sin, no matter who practices it. If God will send a sinner to hell for sinning, how much more ought his children never to practice sin? We Christians ought to be saved from sin.

While I am not one who believes in what some call Christian "perfection", I believe there is such a thing as being cleansed from sin, walking in the Spirit, and not fulfilling the lust of the flesh. I believe it is entirely within the right of any Christian to go to God and demand that God make him holy and keep him from sin. Of course, that Christian may stumble. If they stumble, there is a first-aid kit. "My little children, these things write I unto you, that ye sin not" – that is the will of God, number one. "But if any man sin he has an advocate with the Father" – that is the first-aid kit (1 John 2:1 KJV). The Lord does not let his stumbling children die. He picks them up, dusts them off, binds up their wounds and starts them all anew.

So there is deliverance if we sin, but we should not always make provision for sinning. If we make provision for sinning tomorrow, we will sin tomorrow. But if we go on our knees and say, "Lord, there's nothing good in me but I believe that you are my keeper, my sanctifier and that you will keep me from sin", God will keep us from sin.

Those are the seven tests. I exhort you to press on. If he has done something for you, thank him with all of your heart and "seek those things which are above, where Christ sitteth on the right hand of God" (Colossians 3:1 KJV). The place up there is better than anything that can be down here. There is nothing in this wide world that will be as wonderful as when we look upon his face and see him as he is. If talking with him here is wonderful, how much more wonderful it will be to talk to him without a veil.